NEW FAST CLASS

for First Certificate

Kathy Gude

GW00696843

STUDENT'S BOOK & ONLINE WORKBOOK

OXFORD
UNIVERSITY PRESS

INTRODUCTION

Your *New Fast Class* Student's Book includes access to your *Fast Class Online Workbook* which will boost your exam-taking confidence with:

» Further practice in all the FCE exam skills
» Grammar and vocabulary exercises which revise and build on language covered in your Student's Book
» 100 Key word transformations
» Unit-by-unit wordlists

» Learning support features* like explanatory feedback, *Oxford Advanced Learner's Dictionary* look-up, the *Oxford Learner's Pocket Grammar* reference look-up and exam training tips
» A complete online oxfordenglishtesting.com FCE practice test.

* These features are only available if you use your Online Workbook for self-study or if your teacher sets your Online Workbook assignments in 'Practice mode'. See page 3 for more information.

USING YOUR *NEW FAST CLASS* ONLINE WORKBOOK

There are two options for using your *New Fast Class* Online Workbook:

A Your teacher will select units, sections or exercises of your Online Workbook and assign them for you to do. They will be able to track your progress and see your results.

Your teacher will send you log-in details so you can access your Online Workbook assignments.

OR

B Your teacher will ask you to use the Online Workbook for 'self-study' – you will be able to select any exercises that you want to do.

For registration details see the instructions on the Registration card at the back of this book. You will need an email address to register.

1 After you log in to start using your Online Workbook, click the 'get started' link on your home page. Read the quick-start guide and watch the demo before you start.

2 Click the unit or assignment name in 'Tasks to do' or 'My tasks' to start doing your Online Workbook exercises.

3 Click the link for the exercise you want to work on.

4 When you have answered all the questions in an assignment that your teacher has given you, click 'Submit' on the 'Unit overview' or 'Section summary' to get your work marked.

If you are working through the Online Workbook yourself (i.e. using option B, self-study), you can mark individual questions, exercises, sections or the whole unit, but once you have clicked 'Submit' you won't be able to change your answers.

ONLINE WORKBOOK UNIT CONTENTS

Each of the 10 units contains the following sections:

Reading
Exam-type tasks and vocabulary exercises using texts that relate to unit topics in the Student's Book.

Writing
Exam-type writing tasks that can be marked online by your teacher.

Vocabulary
Exercises to revise and extend vocabulary covered in the Student's Book.

Use of English
Exam type-task.

Grammar
Exercises to revise and extend areas of grammar covered in the Student's Book.

Listening
Exam-type listening tasks.

Speaking
Exercises with audio extracts that focus on useful language and strategies for the Speaking exam.

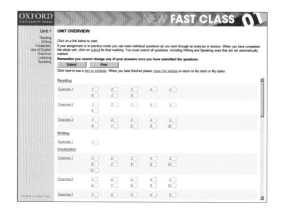

LEARNING SUPPORT FEATURES

Feedback	Get feedback on marked questions. Click the 'Feedback' link at the bottom of your Online Workbook screen to find out why your answer was wrong (or right!). Understanding why you answered a question incorrectly will help you to think more clearly about a similar question the next time.
Dictionary look-up: *Oxford Advanced Learner's Dictionary*	Look up the meaning of words in exercises and texts. Just double click on a word and get a definition from the *OALD* in a pop-up window. This saves you time and helps you improve your vocabulary.
Grammar reference: *Oxford Learner's Pocket Grammar*	Get more information about grammar points covered in grammar exercises. Click on the 'Grammar reference' link at the bottom of your Online Workbook screen to open relevant pages from the *Oxford Learner's Pocket Grammar* by John Eastwood. This increases your confidence in grammar practice.
Tips	Get tips on how to answer exam questions and other general language learning tips. Click 'Show Tip' on the left of your Online Workbook screen.
Audio scripts	Read audio scripts in the Listening and Speaking sections to help you understand any areas you didn't understand when you just listened. Click the 'Audio script' link at the bottom of your Online Workbook screen.
Sample answers	You can see sample answers in the Writing sections after you have written your own answer for an extended writing task (email, essay, etc.) and have clicked 'Mark'. You will be able to read comments on the sample answer to give you a good idea of what is expected in the exam.
Useful language	Get a list of useful language in the Speaking sections. Click the 'Useful language' link at the bottom of your Online Workbook screen for lists of useful expressions for the Speaking exam.
Change your answers and try again	Click the 'Change' button to do an exercise again, or to try to answer a question again. You can do this as many times as you want before you submit your assignment if you are using the self-study option or your teacher has set your assignment in 'Practice mode'. Once you have clicked 'Submit' you cannot change your answers.
Unit-by-unit wordlists	Download or print off unit-by-unit wordlists to complete with translations in your own language. You can use these to test yourself. Click the 'Resources' tab on your home page.

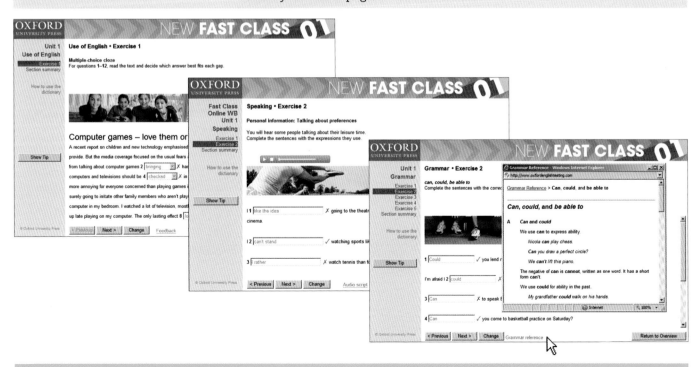

Note that these features are only available if you use your Online Workbook for the self-study option or if your teacher sets your Online Workbook assignments in 'Practice mode'. You need to enable pop-up windows in your browser.

CONTENTS

WRITING GUIDE Page 116 **EXAM OVERVIEW** Page 124

MULTIPLE CHOICE

1 **Discuss the questions.**

a What do you think makes a film successful?

b Which do you think is more important in a film: the story or the special effects? Why?

2 **Read the article quickly and find out what Gareth Edwards does for a living.**

> What films that you have seen have the best
> a) special effects? b) background music? c) story?
> d) acting?
> Why do you think that some good films are not
> box-office successes, but some bad films are?

250,000 SOLDIERS? NO PROBLEM!

Will Hodgson meets the director outdoing Hollywood in his own bedroom.

1 So you've just shot a major battle scene for your historical epic, but you don't like the hill in the background. What do you do? Simple: find a hill somewhere else. 'I searched for "hill" on the internet and got about 1,000 images,' says
5 Gareth Edwards, the British film-maker who created all 250 of the frequently breathtaking special effects for his new television drama, *Attila the Hun*. And he did it all on a computer in his London flat! 'None of them were right though, so I ended up using a hill from an old photograph.'

10 *Attila the Hun* marks a revolution in film-making. The hour-long feature film, made for only the cost of an average documentary, was filmed over three weeks in Bulgaria, has a small cast, and is receiving practically no promotion. Yet, through a combination of new, affordable
15 software and a lot of talent on the part of the director, *Attila* has battle scenes and ancient landscapes to match the *Lord of the Rings* or *Gladiator*.

Edwards demonstrates how he created the final battle scene for *Attila*, which has a quarter of a million Huns and
20 Romans fighting. For the Huns, Edwards shot just four men in a variety of positions – running, attacking, etc. – against a green background. He multiplied the men, asked the computer to create light and dark shades on them, and varied the speed of their movements. Hey presto – he
25 had an army. Then he added them to the scenes shot in Bulgaria, along with his specially-constructed hill.

The Roman army, meanwhile, was even cheaper: it consisted of just one man. 'The strange thing is, the fewer people you use, the more realistic your army is,'
30 says Edwards. 'If you have two people, you notice the difference between them, but with one figure in different positions, you just accept that that was what Roman soldiers looked like. A Hollywood film would shoot 600 guys and see which ones work. My attitude is to do the
35 opposite: I pick the laziest option, and if that works, I then move on to the next scene.'

Just as George Lucas created his breakthrough film *THX 1138* using little more than a handful of actors in white corridors, so Edwards is beginning to produce
40 inexpensive, epic-scale film-making that requires little more than a vivid imagination and a skilled hand on a computer mouse. Over the five months it took him to make *Attila*, Edwards often worked through the night to colour castles and multiply attacking armies using software
45 programs. 'Doing this makes you a bit strange,' he says, as he shows me how to break up a castle wall. 'You can easily end up having social problems!'

Edwards says he has never had any interest in computers in their own right; he has simply been quick to realise
50 what they can do. 'All I wanted to do was plug a wire directly into my brain and press "record",' he says of his early days in film-making. 'But I discovered that even shooting a street scene for a few seconds with a crew can take thousands of pounds and miles of red tape. For that
55 reason, visual effects seemed like the most powerful tool to get involved in. One day, computers will solve all the logistic problems associated with filming.'

Attila works as a traditional piece of storytelling and as historical recreation, with little in it to suggest a triumph
60 of computer manipulation. This is both Edwards' reward and problem: if he does his job right, all of his hard work goes unnoticed. 'People call this CGI (computer-generated images),' he says. 'That gives the impression that only computers created it. But all that matters is making the
65 film that is in your head.'

Part 1: Multiple choice

» Quickly read the title and the extract for gist.

» Even if you think you know the answer, check all the options.

3 **Read the article again. For questions 1–8, choose the answer (A, B, C or D) which you think fits best according to the text.**

1 How did Gareth create the hill in his battle scene?

  A He used an image he found on the internet.

  B He drew the hill using computer software.

  C He copied a suitable hill from a photograph he had.

  D He took a photograph himself of a nearby hill.

2 What does the writer say about the film *Attila the Hun*?

  A It received a lot of publicity.

  B It was a very low-budget film.

  C It cannot match the quality of some other films.

  D It took a long period of time to produce.

3 What comment does the writer make about filming the Huns for the final battle scene?

  A Thousands of actors were used.

  B The whole army was placed against light and dark backgrounds.

  C The battle scenes were speeded up after they had been filmed.

  D A few soldiers were filmed doing several different things.

4 Why does the writer use the expression 'Hey presto' in line 24?

  A to emphasise the problems involved in shooting the battle scene

  B to highlight how quickly the army had been created in one battle scene

  C to show how difficult it can be to make a battle look realistic

  D to explain the need to film the soldiers in different positions

5 What does Gareth suggest about cinema audiences in paragraph 4?

  A They can be quite easily fooled by what they are watching.

  B They can easily lose their concentration when watching a film.

  C They know exactly what characters should look like.

  D They notice details directors might not expect them to be aware of.

6 What comment does Gareth make about his job in paragraph 5?

  A Anyone who is good with computers could do it.

  B It takes up very little of his own free time.

  C It's not a normal kind of thing that he is doing.

  D He has no problems finding people to socialise with.

7 What reason does Gareth give for doing what he does now?

  A He is still passionately interested in computers.

  B He finds ordinary film-making too time-consuming and expensive.

  C He is able to make a lot of money out of film-making.

  D He has got rid of all the problems involved with making films.

8 What conclusion does the writer draw about Gareth's work in paragraph 7?

  A It's only successful if no one knows what he has done.

  B It's instantly recognisable as being his own work.

  C It has made a big impact on modern cinema audiences.

  D It is only the start of what he might be able to achieve.

NOUN ENDINGS

4 **Use these endings to make the noun forms of adjectives a–i. You may need to change other letters.**

-ion	-ity	-ment	-ness
-y	-ation	-action	

a real

b unwilling

c disappointed

d determined

e perfect

f generous

g satisfying

h luxurious

i lazy

01 WRITING

INFORMAL TRANSACTIONAL EMAIL

1 Read the exam task and the email, ignoring the notes Carla has made, and find out these things.

   a Why has David sent the email?

   b What would he like Carla to do?

   c What he is looking forward to?

   d What does he want to know?

You have received an email from your penfriend David, who is coming to stay with you for a week. Read his email and the notes you have made. Then write an email to him in 120–150 words in an appropriate style, using your notes.

2 Which of the following is David doing in the email? What words and expressions does he use to do these things?

   – giving information

   – requesting information

   – making a complaint

   – making a suggestion

   – making a request

3 Find informal words or expressions David uses which mean the same as these more formal ones.

   a telephone you

   b waste time waiting for me

   c I'm very excited at the thought of

   d similar kinds of things

   e give me some information

4 Look at the notes Carla has made. What do you think she is going to say in her reply to David's email? Write one sentence for each of her notes.

5 Read Carla's email, ignoring the mistakes. Is it different from what you expected? How?

Hi Carla!

Just a quick email to say I'll be arriving at the end of next month. Could you <u>meet me</u>? Perhaps I can give you a ring about half an hour before I get there so you won't have to wait around for me. Can't wait to see the <u>sights</u> and have a few nights out together. By the way, what sort of <u>clothes</u> should I bring? Will we need swimming things or anything like that? Let me know. What about <u>money</u>? Is everything very expensive or can I get by without breaking the bank?

See you soon

David

train / bus?

Which sights? / what to do?

summer / July usually warm

need lots!

Dear my cousin

I need to know if you are coming by bus or train and what day you arriving. It might be difficult to meet you because I have classes on weekdays. You might have to take a taxi to my house. You mention to see the sights, but not which sights. Dad doesn't like me to staying out too late at night so we have to think of something for earlier in the evening. Clothes are not a problem. You can wear what you like. I can't swim so we won't go swiming. I am exciting that you are coming because we have not seen each other since a long time.

Yours sincerely

Carla

>> Use the *Writing guide* on page 116.

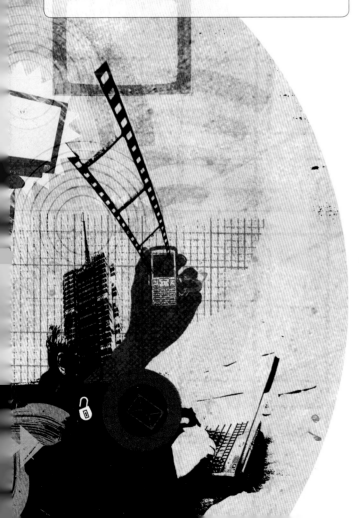

CAN YOU TELL ME …?

6 **What changes do you need to make to the question** *Are you coming by train?* **to begin the question** *Can you tell me … ?*

7 **Rewrite sentences a–i using** *Can you tell me … ?* **You may need to make other changes.**

   a What time does your train arrive?
   b Which hotel are you staying at?
   c Where should I meet you?
   d Do you need somewhere to stay?
   e What would you like to do?
   f Are you interested in opera?
   g Would you like to go on a river trip?
   h When's your return flight?
   i Are you a vegetarian?

EXPRESSIONS WITH *WAY*

8 **Find an expression with** *way* **in David's email. What does it mean? Complete sentences a–f using** *way* **and these words.**

| in the | a long | get her own |
| out of their | find your | on our |

   a I hope you can _____ to my house.
   b I live _____ from the airport.
   c _____ home, we can do some sightseeing.
   d My host family went _____ to make me feel at home.
   e Could you move your suitcases because they're _____?
   f My sister is selfish. She always likes to _____.

WRITING A REPLY

9 **Look at Carla's email again and circle the mistakes.**

10 **Read the exam task in 1 and the notes on David's email again, then write your own reply to David. Try to use some of the structures and expressions in 6–8.**

>> EXAM HELPLINE

Part 1: Informal transactional email

>> You must answer the Part 1 question. It has equal marks with Part 2 so allow enough time for both.

>> Use the right tone for the person reading your email.

>> Check your finished email for sense and errors.

>> Use the *Writing guide* on page 116.

MULTIPLE-CHOICE CLOZE

1 Read the text quickly, ignoring the gaps, and find out what Javier Mollevan was studying.

Interacting with robots

Move over, laptops – it's robots that ^{0}_____ be the next-generation classroom teaching tools! A study ^{1}_____ out by Javier Movellan in San Diego tested four robots by introducing them into a nursery classroom of toddlers aged ^{2}_____ 18 months and 2 years. The team used toddlers instead of older children ^{3}_____ it was easier to focus on the interaction when there was no speech involved. ^{4}_____ the toddlers had become used to the robots, they began to ^{5}_____ them with care and attention – hugging them, helping them when they ^{6}_____ down, and covering them with a blanket when the robot's batteries ran ^{7}_____ . One thing that became clear was the importance of timing. Apparently simply moving the robot's head too slowly or too fast can ^{8}_____ the children behave differently towards the robot. Movellan says the ^{9}_____ of the study prove that we are very close to building robots that might be able to interact with humans in a social manner. The interaction observed between the children and the robots definitely created a ^{10}_____ positive atmosphere in the classroom. Mollevan is careful to point out, ^{11}_____ , that robots could never play the same role as humans. They might be a substitute for pets and toys, and ^{12}_____ to be effective teaching tools, but nothing can replace good, old-fashioned human interaction!

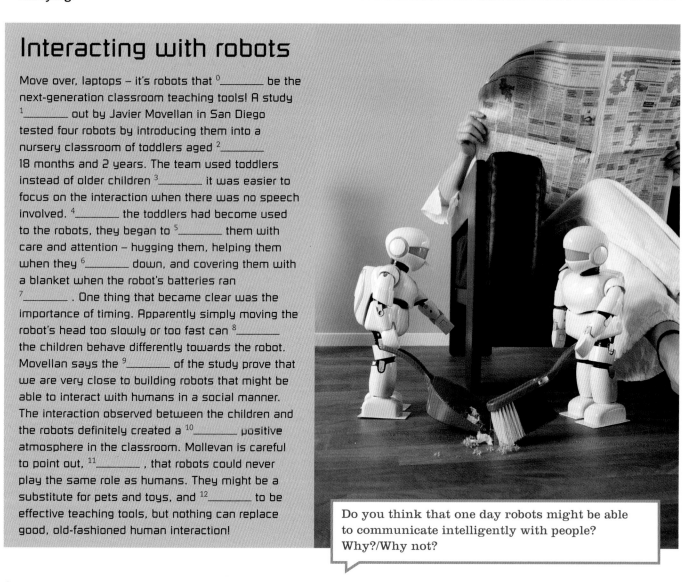

Do you think that one day robots might be able to communicate intelligently with people? Why?/Why not?

2 For questions 1–12, read the text again and decide which answer (A, B, C or D) best fits each gap.

0	A must	B can	C would	D might
1	A handed	B given	C carried	D brought
2	A about	B between	C over	D at
3	A because	B once	C even if	D so that
4	A Before	B Since	C When	D While
5	A regard	B hold	C consider	D treat
6	A fell	B set	C tripped	D pulled
7	A away	B over	C out	D off
8	A bring	B make	C produce	D cause
9	A results	B effects	C decisions	D developments
10	A just	B far	C very	D much
11	A but	B however	C yet	D even
12	A recommend	B suggest	C show	D prove

TEST YOUR KNOWLEDGE: MODALS

Circle three different modals in the text in 1. Which of the statements a–f about modals are true?

a They have no s in the third person singular.

b They can't be used in question tags.

c Most modal verbs are followed by to.

d They are usually used with another verb.

e They are generally used to express feelings or attitudes.

f They don't normally have past forms.

CAN/COULD, BE ABLE TO

3 **In which of sentences a–g do the modals indicate: possibility, ability, a polite request, a suggestion, permission?**

a Could you speak English when you were five years old?

b Can you come swimming with us tonight?

c Could you tell me the time?

d We could go to the cinema tonight.

e You can leave work early today as there's very little to do.

f I suppose Greg could have forgotten our telephone number.

g Were you able to ride a bike when you were a child?

MUST BE/HAVE BEEN, CAN'T BE/HAVE BEEN

4 **Complete sentences a–d using must be/have been or can't be/have been.**

a You _____ feeling well. You haven't eaten your dinner.

b Phil _____ exhausted yesterday. He ran in the marathon.

c You _____ Brian's new flatmate. He told me you'd moved in last week.

d Who broke this window? It _____ the children because they're at school.

MUST/MUSTN'T, HAVE/HAD TO

5 **Use must/mustn't or have/had to to complete sentences a–d. More than one answer may be possible.**

a People _____ smoke in the library.

b _____ we _____ hand in this homework tomorrow, or can we have more time?

c I _____ send my grandmother a card. She'll be upset if I forget her birthday.

d I _____ get up really early this morning to go to football practice.

MAY (NOT), MIGHT (NOT), CAN/COULD (NOT)

6 **Complete sentences a–d. More than one answer may be possible.**

a It _____ rain this afternoon. There are some dark clouds over there.

b _____ I use your phone?

c Paul _____ have received the email. I'll call him.

d Sorry we _____ come to your party.

MUSTN'T, NEEDN'T, NOT HAVE TO

7 **Complete sentences a–c. Which two modals can have the same meaning?**

a You _____ do the homework tonight. You can hand it in on Friday.

b You _____ be late for work on your first day. It creates a very bad impression.

c We _____ buy train tickets at the station – they sell them on the train.

SHOULD (DO)/HAVE (DONE), OUGHT TO (DO)/HAVE (DONE)

8 **Use these verbs and the correct form of the words in brackets to complete sentences a–d.**

go	be	begin	take

a We _____ (should) to look for a hotel much earlier. We'll never find one now.

b The plane _____ (ought) off soon. It was due to leave ten minutes ago.

c We _____ (ought) somewhere different for our holidays. We were bored doing the same things.

d The children _____ (should) in bed by now. It's nearly 9 o'clock.

DIDN'T NEED TO, DIDN'T HAVE TO, NEEDN'T HAVE

9 **Complete sentences a–d using didn't need to, didn't have to or needn't have and the verbs in brackets. More than one answer may be possible.**

a My brother _____ (take) a taxi after the party because someone gave him a lift.

b It was kind of you to telephone, but you _____ (go) to all that trouble.

c I _____ (be) at school until 10.30 yesterday morning so I had a lie-in.

d We _____ (worry) about being late. When we got there no other guests had arrived.

WORDS WITH DIFFERENT MEANINGS

1 Read through the questions and options in 2 below. Decide which meaning, (a or b), is most likely for these words from each extract.

1 past
  a long ago
  b after

2 steps
  a stairs
  b parts of a process

3 in the way of
  a be an obstacle
  b regarding

4 order
  a request
  b command

5 the nerve
  a part of the body
  b the courage

6 unwind
  a undo
  b take it easy

7 customs
  a ways of behaving
  b officials at borders

8 company
  a business or firm
  b being with a person

MULTIPLE CHOICE

≫ EXAM HELPLINE

Part 1: Multiple choice

≫ You hear each situation and question, then a pause, so concentrate on one question at a time.

≫ Don't worry if you hear unknown words. Think about the overall meaning.

2 (◎ 1) **You will hear people talking in eight different situations. For questions 1–8, choose the best answer (A, B or C).**

1 A couple who have just moved house are talking to each other. What is the man complaining about?
  A moving the furniture
  B having to unpack
  C missing lunch

2 You hear a tourist guide talking about some old houses. Who were they built for?
  A the general public
  B company employees
  C servants

3 A woman approaches a man outside a railway station. What does she want him to do?
  A take part in a survey
  B fill in a questionnaire
  C give her some personal details

4 You hear the recorded message of a holiday company. What can you do if you press 2?
  A ask for a brochure
  B speak to an operator
  C enquire about a previous booking

5 You hear part of a radio interview with an author. How does the author feel now?
  A misunderstood
  B bitter
  C nervous

6 A doctor is talking about long-distance flying. What does she say passengers should do?
  A keep to their normal routine
  B only eat a little when on board
  C relax after landing

7 While at the post office, you hear a man talking. What is he worried about?
  A the cost of posting his parcel
  B how to send his parcel
  C losing his parcel

8 You hear an advertisement on the radio. What is special about the products on offer?
  A They are good value.
  B They are easy to handle.
  C They are elegant.

3 **Which meanings did the words in 1 have?**

Have you ever moved house? What problems did you have?

Have you ever bought something advertised on the radio, TV or internet? What? Were you satisfied?

01 SPEAKING

PERSONAL INFORMATION

1 Tick the subjects you think the examiner might ask you about in Part 1 of the speaking test.

home

neighbourhood

family

environmental problems

future plans

making decisions

favourite day of the week

hobbies and interests

comparing photographs

jobs

studying English

your partner's photographs

past experiences

feelings

» EXAM HELPLINE

Part 1: Personal information

» Part 1 lasts three minutes for two students and five minutes for groups of three.

» Try not to be too nervous – smile, take a deep breath, and start speaking.

» Speak loudly and clearly enough for both examiners to hear you.

» If you have no plans, interests or hobbies, etc., explain why, e.g. 'because I have no time'.

2 Sentences a–g all contain at least one mistake. Say them correctly.

a I am coming from the Spain.

b I was grown up in city.

c I am enjoying to live in my neighbourhood.

d I'm student at the technical college.

e I've been study English since six years.

f I like very much the sports, on particular, tennis.

g I'm interested on computers.

3 Look again at the sentences you corrected in 2. What questions would you ask someone to find out this information?

4 Read this conversation between a candidate and an examiner. Why are Pierre's answers unsuitable? How could they be improved?

Pierre, do you live in town?

No, I don't.

Where are you from?

A village.

What do you like about living there?

It's quiet.

5 With a partner, use the subjects you ticked in 1 to ask and answer questions about yourself. Expand on your answers with an extra piece of information.

Example: *I'm really interested in computers. I spend a lot of time surfing the internet and sending emails to my friends.*

EXPRESSIONS WITH *PICK* Extension p6 text

1 What does the word *pick* mean in the text on page 6 (line 35)? Match a–e with the meanings 1–5.

a pick on someone

b pick someone's pocket

c pick a fight or quarrel

d pick up speed

e pick your way

1 cause an argument with someone deliberately

2 move slowly or carefully, avoiding obstacles

3 criticise someone unfairly

4 steal money from someone's clothing

5 go faster

2 Use the correct form of the expressions in 1 to complete sentences a–e.

a I don't like Brian. He's always trying to _____ with the other boys in the class.

b You shouldn't _____ people who are weaker than you are.

c The car _____ as it travelled downhill.

d Someone _____ on the train yesterday and stole all my money.

e The children _____ across the beach, which was covered in pebbles.

NEGATIVE PREFIXES FOR OPPOSITE MEANINGS Extension p6 text

3 Find the negative of *expensive* in the text on page 6. Write words which mean the opposite of the words in a–j, using the prefixes *un-*, *im-*, *in-* or *dis-*.

a perfect

b appear

c fasten

d polite

e like (verb)

f like (adjective)

g correct (adjective)

h necessary

i exact

j realistic

PHRASAL VERBS WITH *UP* Extension p6 text

4 What do *break up* and *end up* mean in the text on page 6? Match the phrasal verbs with *up* in sentences a–f with the meanings 1–6.

a David has *picked up* French really quickly.

b You'll have to work hard to *keep up* with the rest of the class.

c Guess who *turned up* at Paul's party the other night!

d Where were you *brought up*?

e They've just *put* the price of petrol *up* again.

f If it *clears up* later, we can go for a walk.

1 learn

2 increase

3 arrive unexpectedly

4 stop raining

5 raise children

6 maintain the same standard as

NOUN ENDINGS Extension p7 ex 4

5 Make the verbs in a–i into nouns using the endings
-ion, -ation, -tion, -ment, -ence, or -ary.

a demonstrate

b differ

c construct

d imagine

e produce

f move

g document

h embarrass

i explain

CAN YOU TELL ME ...? Revision p9 ex 6–7

6 Rewrite a–f beginning Can you tell me ... ?

a Where's the railway station?

b Do you like opera?

c What are you going to study at university?

d Who are you writing to?

e Are you going to the seminar on Saturday?

f Would you like to study another language?

WRITING Extension p8/9

7 Write an email to a friend inviting him/her to come
and stay with you for the weekend. Remember to

- tell your friend where and when you will meet
  them.

- explain what you are planning to do at the weekend.

- ask your friend what he/she might like to do.

MODALS Revision p11

8 Use the verb in brackets and the correct form of a
suitable modal to complete sentences a–f. More than
one answer may be possible.

a Unfortunately, my boyfriend _____ (go) on
holiday with us next month.

b We _____ (revise) for our exams instead of
watching TV last night.

c This picture _____ (paint) by Picasso. I
recognise his style.

d The food in the fridge _____ (eat)
yesterday. It's past its sell-by date!

e You really _____ (buy) me a present, but it
was very kind of you.

f Everyone _____ (try) to concentrate more
in class.

9 Correct the mistakes in sentences a–g.

a Students might not be late for lessons.

b We couldn't be able to go to the cinema tomorrow
night.

c Ted might have be held up in the traffic. He isn't
usually late.

d Luggage must not to be left unattended.

e Do we must finish this homework by tomorrow?

f When I woke up, I can hear the birds singing.

g I didn't had to wait long for a train last night.

10 Choose the best answer (a, b, c or d) to complete
sentences 1–7.

1 You _____ be tired! You didn't get out of bed until
midday.
a must   b ought   c can't   d should

2 It _____ snow tomorrow.
a can   b couldn't   c might   d needn't

3 We _____ to get up early tomorrow morning.
a need   b haven't   c can't   d must

4 My aunt _____ to have had her operation by now.
a must   b ought   c can't   d should

5 You _____ have come to stay with us last weekend
when you were in town.
a should   b can   c need   d had to

6 The students _____ worried about their end-of-
term test. They all passed.
a didn't need to   b needn't have
c didn't have to   d shouldn't have to

7 I _____ left my book on the train. I can't find it.
a couldn't have   b can't have
c had to   d might have

QUESTION TAGS WITH MODALS
Extension p11

11 Use suitable question tags to complete a–h.

a Sky diving can be dangerous, _____?

b Ted could have phoned, _____?

c Mary shouldn't have said that, _____?

d Richard had to leave the party early, _____?

e We didn't need to write two essays, _____?

f They must have missed the bus, _____?

g Your parents might have phoned while we were out,
_____?

h We have to be there at 9 o'clock, _____?

MISSING SENTENCES

1 In some countries, students do a few weeks' work experience while they are still at school. Discuss the questions.

a Do you or would you like to have this in your country?

b How useful do you think this is? What could you learn from it?

2 Read the article, ignoring the gaps. What do you think the writer learnt from his work experience in France?

›› EXAM HELPLINE

Part 2: Missing sentences

›› Read the main text for gist to identify what kind of information is missing.

›› Read sentences A–H and find words which refer to something in the main text.

3 Read the article again. Seven sentences have been removed. Choose from the sentences A–H the one which fits each gap (1–7). There is one extra sentence which you do not need to use.

A The whole ordeal of either kissing or shaking hands with everybody but the dog became routine.

B I am sure that in my oral exam in the summer, they will be the only words I can recall.

C There had been a slight problem with the computers at the newspaper.

D I had made it through a week that had started in the worst possible way and seemed designed to get even worse.

E And so it was to my surprise that early the next day I found myself sheepishly standing in a farmyard in hastily-borrowed clothes and boots two sizes too big.

F In rural France, there is no tea break at eleven, the midday meal takes up twice as long – and starts an hour earlier.

G What little that remained was shrinking as fast as the docks were fading into obscurity.

H I discovered that it is really not all it is cracked up to be, and no more exciting than driving a car.

> How would you feel if you were leaving home to go and work in another country for a few weeks?
>
> What would people find unusual about living and working in your country for a short time?

HAVE YOU HEARD THE MOOS?

1 **How 17-year-old Henry Bainton's work experience at a French local newspaper turned into a crash course in farming.**

5 As Portsmouth drifted into the horizon, it seemed as if almost every useful word of French I had ever learnt was left behind on the quayside. **1** ☐ It dawned on me that this was really the point of no return. The
10 very next day I would be working in France, writing in French on a local newspaper and living with a family that was not my own.

I was well prepared for my stay – and I had been looking forward to it. My suit was
15 pressed, my shoes polished, and my white shirts meticulously ironed. A hint of suspicion crept in though when, having arrived in the picturesque town of Flers, where we were based, my teacher tactfully informed me
20 that there was a 'minor hitch'. **2** ☐ 'Never mind,' I thought, 'I've already had some experience of a newsroom in England, and I'm sure a French newsroom can't be that different so I won't be missing too much.'
25 'You have brought your wellies though, haven't you?' asked the teacher.

I had little more with me than a suit carrier and a toothbrush. **3**☐ This was the replacement placement – a farm. I felt like the new boy in
30 the class all over again – with unfamiliar faces staring at me with an air of superiority. I had never been in such close proximity to a cow before, but I conceded in the end that they were far less bothered by me than I was by them,
35 and realised that a peaceful coexistence would probably be possible.

I was informed that work would start at a reasonable hour of the day. **4**☐ Nor was lunch just a sandwich at the canteen – only the
40 farm's own roast meat, home-made patisserie and home-brewed cider would suffice after a morning in the fields.

Having aspired from the age of three to drive a tractor, I finally made it aboard the farm's
45 latest purchase, a £300,000 Lamborghini tractor. My mind boggled at the complexity and cost of the gleaming new machine whose engine roared with so much as a tap on the gas pedal. **5**☐ But it is nice to be able to claim that I have
50 driven one.

French customs felt progressively less alien as the week went on. **6**☐ And I even found myself developing an interest in French sporting successes and fashions. Spending all
55 that time with French teenagers, immersed in the language, meant taking in all those words that would shock my bilingual teacher. But by the end of the week, I had even started to dream in French.
60 After all that had happened, it was a sigh of both relief and pathos that I breathed when we at last steamed away from Caen. **7**☐ And above all, I learnt a great deal – not only the hundred or so different expressions to shout at a
65 misbehaving dog, but I also gained a genuine impression of how the French live.

PHRASAL VERBS WITH *TAKE*

4 Complete the phrasal verbs in sentences a–f with these words. Then match them with the meanings 1–6.

up	over	in	back
away	after		

a The teacher spoke so quickly that I couldn't take _____ what he was saying.

b This homework is taking _____ the whole day.

c Don't you think Lisa takes _____ her mother?

d What do you get if you take this number _____ from that one?

e I think I will take these shoes _____ to the shop. They don't fit properly.

f I hear that an American company is taking _____ the organisation.

1 occupy (space or time)
2 subtract or remove
3 follow or understand
4 get control of
5 resemble
6 return

CONFUSING WORDS

5 At least one of the verbs in these pairs appears in the text. Use the pairs in their correct form to complete sentences a and b in 1–6.

gain/win	realise/understand
lend/borrow	expect/look forward to
stare/glance	stay/remain

1 a Could you _____ me some money for lunch today?
  b I'll _____ some money from my sister.

2 a Not much food _____ on the table after the party.
  b Please come and _____ with us next week.

3 a Do you _____ people who speak French to you?
  b I didn't _____ how much French I knew.

4 a I didn't _____ work experience to be fun.
  b I am _____ going to London in the spring.

5 a Who _____ the last World Cup?
  b Students can _____ a lot from travelling.

6 a It's rude to _____ at people!
  b Paul _____ quickly through the magazine.

FORMAL TRANSACTIONAL LETTER

1 Read the exam task and the letter, ignoring Martin's notes. Correct any information in a–c which is false.

a Anyone can go to the student conference.

b If you wish to go to the conference, you must write a letter to the head teacher.

c Most of the cost of the trip will be financed by the parents.

Your school is organising a trip to an international student conference in Spain. Read the letter sent out to students and the notes you have made.

2 Read Martin's reply to the head teacher's letter on page 19. Has he included all the notes he made on the letter?

FORMAL AND INFORMAL WORDS

3 Martin is having problems finding the right kind of formal language to use. Choose the words or phrases a–m to replace those underlined in his letter.

a reply

b handing it in

c helpful

d to receive

e look forward to receiving

f in the near future

g participating in

h am convinced

i finally

j could you possibly tell me

k information

l an indication

m mentioned

Dear students

I am writing to inform you of an exciting event which will take place <u>next year</u>. The school has been asked to send six delegates to take part in the Second International Student Conference in Spain. If you would like to attend the conference, all you have to do is write a 200-word essay entitled 'The Importance of International Cooperation' and <u>hand it in</u> to the school secretary.

The prize for the six best entries, which will be judged by a panel of teachers, will be an expenses-paid trip to the conference, but we will be asking for <u>a small contribution</u> from the parents of the winners.

We very much hope you will be <u>interested</u> in this event, and we look forward to receiving your entries.

Yours sincerely

G Samson

George Samson, Head Teacher

When exactly?

What's the deadline?

How much?

definitely!

ASKING FOR INFORMATION

4 Complete the gaps in sentence openers a–e using these words, then use them to write questions to find out the information in 1–5. More than one answer may be possible.

let	useful	like	concerned	grateful

a I would _____ to know whether …

b Could you possibly _____ me know which … ?

c I would be _____ if you could tell me whether …

d It would be _____ to know whether …

e As far as (the cost) is _____, how much … ?

1 Cost of travelling to Spain?

2 Travelling by coach or train?

3 Need to prepare anything?

4 Parents allowed to accompany children?

5 Languages spoken at the conference?

Dear Mr Samson

I was pleased [1]to get your letter about the competition. I would be very interested in [2]joining this trip, but I would like to find out some more [3]things about the trip.

First of all, [4]do you have any idea exactly when the conference will take place? You also mentioned writing an essay. It would be [5]nice to know what the deadline for [6]giving it to the secretary is. [7]The last thing, you [8]wrote something about a contribution from the parents of the winners. Could you give me [9]a rough idea of how much this might be?

I [10]want to receive your [11]answer [12]quickly so that I can begin to prepare my entry for the competition, which I [13]think will be an interesting experience for the winners.

Yours sincerely

Martin Mouchel

LINK WORDS

5 Complete this paragraph from a parent's letter to the head teacher. Use these link words in suitable places.

but also	Finally	Besides this	Firstly
not only	In addition		

[1]_____, I am delighted that my son has been chosen to take part in the conference. [2]_____, I would like to say what an excellent idea it is. The students chosen to attend will [3]_____ enjoy the experience, [4]_____ they will learn something useful. [5]_____, it will give them a chance to travel to another country and meet people from all over the world. [6]_____, may I congratulate you on organising the event and encouraging students to be aware of the importance of international cooperation.

EXPRESSIONS WITH *TAKE*

6 Match the expressions with *take* in sentences a–h with meanings 1–8. Which two expressions are in the headmaster's letter in 1?

a You should *take care of* yourself.
b I would very much like to *take part in* the conference.
c Writing a good essay *takes time*.
d The conference will *take place* next month.
e My new book is beginning to *take shape*.
f You should *take advantage of* any chance to travel.
g Doing physical exercise really *takes it out of* you.
h It's important to *take it easy* once in a while.

1 participate in
2 develop into something definite
3 relax
4 make use of or get benefit from
5 cannot be rushed
6 happen
7 look after
8 exhaust

WRITING A REPLY

7 Read the exam task in 1 again and write a suitable reply to the head teacher, including all the information in notes a–d below. Write 120–150 words in an appropriate style. Try to use some of the sentence openers in 4 and the link words in 5.

a venue – city/countryside?
b transport – plane/train?
c accommodation – hotel/host family?
d essay – hand-written/typed?

>> EXAM HELPLINE

Part 1: Formal transactional letter

>> Transactional letters appear in Part 1. Non-transactional letters appear in the questions in Part 2.

>> Read the input material carefully so that you include all the points asked for in the question.

>> Use the *Writing guide* on page 117.

OPEN CLOZE

1 Read the text quickly, ignoring the gaps. Find out how many languages there are in the world. How many are spoken by more than 100 million people?

2 For questions 1–12, read the text again and think of the word which best fits each gap. Use only one word in each gap.

» EXAM HELPLINE

Part 2: Open cloze

» Quickly read the title and the text for gist.

» The sentence before or after each gap may help you to find out the missing word.

» The missing word must fit grammatically and make sense in the context.

LANGUAGES IN DANGER

It appears that 90% of the world's languages are likely to disappear in the next half century, **0** <u>according</u> to research conducted recently. One such language is Tofa, which is only spoken by about 60 people who live in central Siberia. The language **1** _____ also spoken by Manchester University's Gregory Anderson, who is fluent enough to be **2** _____ to express what he wants to say.

Academics from the university are holding an 'Endangered Languages Day' tomorrow. They **3** _____ play videos of native speakers and talk about **4** _____ own field trips around the globe to investigate languages ranging from Faroese, with 50,000 speakers, to Banawa, one of 300 languages spoken in the Amazon Basin.

There is **5** _____ shortage of languages in the world: at the last count, **6** _____ were about 6,000 – but 4% of them are spoken by 96% of the world's people. About 10 languages, **7** _____ English, Arabic and Hindi, are spoken by more than 100 million people each, so there is little need to worry **8** _____ them. On the other **9** _____, languages with a slim chance of survival need help. A language survives **10** _____ it can be transmitted from parents to children. Every language counts because it is the storehouse of the culture of the people **11** _____ speak it. As **12** _____ as the last speaker of a language is lost, the cultural memory of a people is gone forever.

TEST YOUR KNOWLEDGE: PRESENT TENSES

Choose the correct form of the verbs to complete sentences a–f.

a I *believe / am believing* that every country should have its own language.

b The sun *always sets / is always setting* in the west.

c What *do you think / are you thinking* about?

d The children *play / are playing* football now.

e Term *begins / is beginning* next Monday.

f I *meet / am meeting* my friend tomorrow.

PRESENT SIMPLE AND PRESENT CONTINUOUS

3 Match the examples of the present simple and present continuous in sentences a–f with the uses 1–6.

a Peter is revising for his exams.

b Lessons begin at 8.30.

c My mother drives to work.

d The sun rises in the east.

e My younger sister is always borrowing my clothes.

f It is becoming more and more expensive to rent a flat nowadays.

1 This happens regularly.

2 This happens on a regular basis and is annoying.

3 This is an event on a timetable.

4 This implies that something is slowly changing.

5 This is a scientific fact.

6 This is happening at the moment.

PRESENT SIMPLE OR CONTINUOUS?

4 Which of verbs a–q aren't usually used in the continuous form?

a believe
b cry
c hate
d forget
e know
f remember
g leave
h mean
i own
j prefer
k read
l like
m seem
n smell
o understand
p want
q work

5 Use the verbs in brackets in the present simple or continuous to complete sentences a–g.

a What _____ you _____ (eat)? It _____ (smell) terrible!

b It always _____ (rain) in May.

c _____ you _____ (know) the answer to this question?

d Where _____ you _____ (usually/do) your shopping at the weekend?

e Jackie _____ (study) mathematics at university.

f The half term holiday _____ (begin) on Friday 14th.

g Mario _____ (have) dinner with Helen tomorrow.

THE CORRECT ACTIVE OR PASSIVE FORM OF THE PRESENT

6 Put the verbs in brackets into the correct form of the present simple or continuous, active or passive.

a We _____ (study) Spanish in class this year.

b To keep a record of this rare language, words _____ (write) down and _____ (transfer) to a computer.

c You _____ (speak) too quickly for me. Could you slow down a little?

d My sister and I _____ (give) Russian lessons at the moment by a friend of the family.

e Chinese _____ (say) to be a difficult language to learn.

f I am supposed to be working today, but I _____ (feel) too ill.

USING ADVERBS

7 Complete sentences a–e so that they are true for you. Add extra words and use the adverbs in brackets in the correct position.

a I drink _____ and eat _____ for breakfast. (generally)

b I get up _____ in the morning. (sometimes)

c I get home at about _____ on weekdays. (always)

d I forget to _____ when I leave the house. (never)

e I _____ at the weekends. (hardly ever)

8 All the adverbs in 7 can come between the subject and the verb. Which two adverbs can also come at the beginning of the sentence?

IMPROVING YOUR SPELLING

1 (○ 2) **Listen and write words and phrases a–j. If you don't know how to spell them, guess.**

a _____

b _____

c _____

d _____

e _____

f _____

g _____

h _____

i _____

j _____

SENTENCE COMPLETION

2 **Read sentences 1–10 in the exam task below and decide what part of speech is needed to complete them.**

You will hear radio presenter Joan Westwood interviewing Peter Daniels, a student who has worked as a volunteer on a research ship. For questions 1–10, complete the sentences.

3 (○ 3) **Listen to the recording and try to pencil in the right answer for sentences 1–10.**

≫ EXAM HELPLINE

Part 2: Sentence completion

≫ Remember that the words you need to write are words that you actually hear on the tape. You do not need to paraphrase what you hear.

≫ On the second listening, check that your answers make sense in the context.

4 (○ 3) **Now listen again. Check the answers you have written for sentences 1–10. What part of speech are most of the correct answers?**

Would you like to do volunteer work on a research ship? Why?/Why not?

Why do you think whale watching has become so popular?

Peter says that seeing whales can make people
¹_____ or even cry.

He thinks people feel great when they see whales because they're very ²_____ animals.

Almost ³_____ a day take part in whale watching.

Because of their size, whales are more
⁴_____ to watch than other creatures.

Some people have sold their ⁵_____ to help raise the money for research into whales.

The interviewer compares whale-watching trips to
⁶_____.

Peter suggests that fewer ⁷_____ should be involved in activities connected with whales.

The aim of whale-watching tour operators is to
⁸_____ tourists.

Whale watching provides ⁹_____ for local people.

The Whale Watching Society is ¹⁰_____ at 17 Green Street, in Halifax.

A VOLUNTEER JOB ON A RESEARCH SHIP

SPEAKING

THE LONG TURN

1 Read the exam task and underline what you think are the most important words.

The photographs show people working in the media. I'd like you to compare the photographs and say what you think it would be like to do these jobs.

2 Look at the two photos and add your own ideas to the list of points to mention below.

Points to mention

Things that are similar about the photos, e.g. both people involved in the news, reaching a large audience.

_____

_____

Things that are different about the photos, e.g. studio and outdoor environment.

_____

_____

3 The examiner asks the listening candidate a short question after his/her partner's turn. Look at the exam task in 1 and the photos in 2. Which of these questions do you think the listening candidate might be asked?

a *What problems do you think people might have doing jobs like these?*

b *Which job would you prefer to do?*

c *Why do you think people enjoy working in the media?*

4 You and a partner are going to do the exam task in 1, but with the pairs of photos on pages 106 and 107. First, make a list of points to mention for each pair. Ignore the questions below the photos.

≫ EXAM HELPLINE

Part 2: The long turn

≫ Listen carefully to the exam task and refer to the questions above the photos if you forget what to do.

≫ Look quickly at both photos and think of three or four things to say.

≫ When answering a question after your partner's long turn, keep your response brief (20 seconds).

5 Take it in turns to talk about the pairs of photos on pages 106 and 107.

Student A Using the linkers below and the lists you made in 4, talk about your pair of photos for one minute.

Student B Stop your partner after one minute and briefly answer the question below your partner's photos.

Comparing photos

Both pictures … , but the first one … .

In this picture … , but in this one … .

This one … . On the other hand, the second one … .

This looks easier/more difficult/enjoyable because … .

TALKING ABOUT THOUGHTS AND FEELINGS

Extension p16/17 text

1 Choose the correct meaning (a, b or c) for the words in italics from the text on pages 16–17.

1 It *dawned on me* …
   a came into my head
   b began to develop in my mind   c seemed to me

2 a hint of *suspicion* crept in …
   a belief   b jealousy   c doubt

3 I *conceded* in the end that …
   a believed   b found out   c admitted

4 … they were far less *bothered by* me …
   a confident about   b worried about   c angry with

5 *My mind boggled* …
   a I was excited   b I was annoyed
   c I became nervous

WORDS CONNECTED WITH WORK

Extension p16/17 text

2 Use these words to complete sentences a–h.

promotion	salary	staff	career
qualifications	job	employers	work

a His twenty-year _____ as a government minister came to an end after the scandal.

b Gardening in this heat is really hard _____.

c The chances of _____ are good if you work hard.

d What kind of _____ do you think you can earn as an engineer?

e _____ should always look after the interests of their workers.

f What _____ do you need to be a doctor?

g Relationships between _____ and management can sometimes be difficult.

h I don't want a _____ with a lot of responsibility.

VERBS AND MEANINGS Extension p16/17 text

3 Match verbs a–g with the speakers' words in 1–7.

a inform   e advise
b threaten   f promise
c claim   g suggest
d deny

1 I didn't say that – it's not true!

2 Of course I'll bring you back a present!

3 If you don't stop criticising me, I'll never speak to you again.

4 Let's go for a pizza!

5 You ought to get more exercise.

6 I'm the best athlete in the school.

7 Dinner is served at seven o'clock.

WRITING Extension p16/17 text

4 Write a paragraph about an experience which you did not enjoy at first, but which you benefited from. Say

– what you did.
– how you felt about your experience.
– what you learned from it.

PHRASAL VERBS WITH *TAKE* Extension p17 ex4

5 Match the phrasal verbs in the pairs of sentences with these pairs of possible meanings.

> remove/leave the ground   adapt yourself to/like
>
> accept an offer/start a hobby

1 a William has been much fitter since he took up running last year.

   b I have decided not to take up the job in Spain.

2 a We took off half an hour late this morning.

   b Would you like to take off your coat?

3 a I didn't take to our new neighbours at first.

   b The twins have taken to tennis like ducks to water!

EXPRESSIONS WITH *COUNT* Extension p20 text

6 What does *at the last count* mean in the text on page 20? Match the words in italics in sentences a–f with the meanings 1–6.

   a Every language in the world *counts*.

   b The marks for this test don't *count towards* the final exam result.

   c We'll have to *count the cost* of not protecting the environment.

   d If you're going to the cinema tonight, you can *count me in*.

   e I'm *counting on* you to help me with this project.

   f I've *lost count of* the number of times I've seen this film.

1 rely

2 suffer the consequences

3 not remember the exact number

4 be important

5 include

6 be included in something (not yet obtained)

PRESENT SIMPLE OR CONTINUOUS?

Revision p21 ex 3–6

7 Five of the sentences in a–i contain mistakes. Find and correct them.

   a I'm doing some temporary work at the moment.

   b Are you thinking it'll rain tomorrow?

   c The summer holidays begin on Friday.

   d The sun is always rising in the east.

   e I'm believing we can do something to stop global warming.

   f This city is becoming more and more crowded.

   g I'm going to the dentist tomorrow.

   h Do you meet your friend Susan tonight?

   i You are seeming a bit upset.

8 Use the verbs in brackets in the present simple or continuous to complete sentences a–e.

   a It _____ (snow) and you _____ (not wear) a hat. You'd better go inside.

   b Sally's father _____ (work) for a computer company in town, but he really _____ (not enjoy) his job.

   c It _____ (appear) that they _____ (build) a new supermarket on the outskirts of town.

   d What _____ (you/do) with my computer? You _____ (know) I _____ (not like) you using my things.

   e The flight _____ (leave) at six o'clock. Danny _____ (come) later to take me to the airport.

9 Use the correct form of these verbs to complete 1–8.

> | call | study | stay | repeat |
> |------|-------|------|--------|
> | teach | not understand | have | not enjoy |

My son normally [1] _____ learning languages, but at the moment he [2] _____ a great time learning Japanese. A young Japanese teacher [3] _____ with us for a few months. He [4] _____ people at my son's school Japanese, and we [5] _____ Japanese with him in the evenings. Most of the time I [6] _____ what 'Miki' (that's what we [7] _____ him here) says, but he very kindly [8] _____ it in English!

INFINITIVE FORMS Extension p21 ex6

10 Use these verbs in the correct infinitive form, e.g. *to do, to be done, to be doing*, to complete sentences a–h. More than one answer may be possible.

> | finish | have | know | be |
> |--------|------|------|-----|
> | play | rise | live | preserve |

   a All the world's languages ought _____.

   b We are lucky _____ in such an exciting city.

   c I would like this work _____ by tomorrow.

   d It's impossible _____ what will happen to endangered languages in the future.

   e We're supposed _____ a lesson now, but the teacher hasn't come.

   f Do you know how _____ the guitar?

   g English is said _____ a difficult language to learn.

   h The cost of public transport appears _____ again.

MULTIPLE MATCHING

1 Quickly read the article on page 27 and match these places to A–D.
- Universal Studios
- Sea World
- Kennedy Space Centre Visitor Complex
- Busch Gardens

» EXAM HELPLINE

Part 3: Multiple matching

» Skim read all the texts quickly before starting to do the task.

» Write, e.g. the places, next to the text where they are mentioned to help you.

2 Read the article again. For questions 1–15, choose from the places (A–D). The places may be chosen more than once.

In which place

1 might some secrets be revealed?

2 can you see straight through the bottom of your vehicle?

3 would you be happy if you didn't like queuing?

4 do adults need to forget about reality?

5 can you make a contribution towards helping the natural world?

6 does the ordinary admission ticket cover a very special attraction?

7 do conservationists have the opportunity to do research?

8 have huge numbers of people come from far and wide to see the attractions?

9 do animals play a leading part in a show?

10 are you advised to choose carefully before you go?

11 is there a height restriction on a ride?

12 can you see huge machines?

13 might you see both African animals and dolphins in the same park?

14 can you be introduced to someone who does an exciting and dangerous job?

15 might you find yourself in the past?

Which of the places in Florida would attract you most? Why?
Some people think animals should not be used to entertain people. What's your opinion?

COMPOUND ADJECTIVES

3 Match the compound adjectives a–f from the text with the meanings 1–6.

a *jaw-dropping* encounters

b *fun-loving* dolphins

c a *non-traditional* circus

d a *15-storey* building

e a *fun-filled* day

f *nail-biting* rides

1 happy and lively

2 breathtaking and unexpected

3 with plenty of entertainment

4 new and different

5 really terrifying

6 with many floors

4 Discuss the questions.

a Can you describe a jaw-dropping experience you have had?

b What's your idea of a fun-filled day?

c Would you describe yourself as a fun-loving person? Why?/Why not?

EXPRESSIONS WITH *KICK*

5 Match the expressions with **kick** in sentences a–d with the meanings 1–4.

a Cirque de Mer *kicks off* the line-up.

b I could *kick myself* for not taking the opportunity to travel when I was younger.

c Tim got *kicked out of* the football team because he never turned up to training sessions.

d The food in the hotel was terrible so my father *kicked up a fuss* about it.

1 be dismissed or sent away

2 be very annoyed with yourself

3 cause a disturbance by protesting

4 start

THE BEST IN FLORIDA ENTERTAINMENT

A _____

1 Embark on mankind's ultimate journey and experience a truly uplifting vacation! Just 45 minutes' drive from Orlando is NASA's launch headquarters, located on a huge island wildlife
5 refuge eight times the size of Manhattan. Each year, millions of visitors from across the world make the trek to this centre of technology and discovery, where many great achievements have taken place. At the Visitor Complex, you get the unique chance
10 to tour NASA's launch and landing facilities. You can experience interactive simulators and jaw-dropping encounters with massive rockets, and even have the opportunity to meet a real member of NASA's Astronaut Corps! Admission also includes the new
15 *Shuttle Launch Experience*, the most realistic launch simulator ever created for the public. You will finally get your chance to be an astronaut! Here the sky isn't the limit – it's the beginning.

B _____

Come to the home of movies and look behind
20 the scenes! The attractions are too numerous to mention, but include the following. In *Back to the Future*, you become a passenger travelling through time to bring the hero back to the present. As a trainee agent in *Men In Black*, *Alien Attack*, you'll
25 shoot aliens as you chase them through the streets of New York in a high-tech ride based on the hit movies. Be warned – these aliens fire back, spinning your vehicle out of control! The studios also have a special 'Kid Zone' (parents are allowed to come
30 as long as they bring their imagination with them). The fun of this theme park is being able to understand how Universal Pictures produced some of the effects in their movies, or at least see the effects from close up. The rides are very thematic
35 and the queues can be quite long – the middle of the day and weekends tend to be the most crowded. It's best to pick the rides you want to go on before you arrive, and turn up early.

C _____

This is the world's most popular marine life park. It
40 brings education, research and conservation together with spectacular family entertainment. The entire family can feed a dolphin, pet a stingray and find out about the animals inhabiting our oceans. There is also an impressive line-up of shows. *Cirque de Mer* kicks
45 off the line-up, mixing acrobatics and comedy with special effects in a non-traditional circus. The tricks are performed by fun-loving dolphins, sea lions and killer whales! The park's rescue efforts are presented in the new show *Pets on Stage*, which features a cast
50 of performing pets adopted from animal shelters. In addition to the shows, there is *Kraken*, the only floorless coaster in Orlando, which takes you to the height of a 15-storey building, upside down at 100 kmph! (You must be over 135cm tall to ride.) If you manage to get
55 through that, you can go to the Waterfront, which is a celebration of the sights, sounds and festivities of the most exciting cities by the sea. You can dine on a gourmet pizza in the open air as the 'staff dressed up as Waterfront townspeople' entertain you.

D _____

60 With gardens, wildlife and wild rides, this park is the ideal place for families. There really is something for everyone here. Whether you go to the park to ride some of the best roller coasters in the US, or to see some of the most exotic animals in the world, you will
65 certainly have a fun-filled day. And for every admission ticket bought at the park, a donation is made to the Wildlife Foundation. The park offers steel and wooden roller coasters, and masses of other nail-biting rides. And the great thing about this park is that you don't
70 have to wait in line for ages before you actually get on a ride. The wildlife is very impressive and includes lions, sloths (like in the *Ice Age* movies) and other animals you would normally only be able to see if you went on a safari. One of the star attractions is the dolphin show,
75 but be careful – the closer you sit to the performance, the more likely you are to get wet!

ARTICLE

1 Decide which one of definitions a–f best describes an article?

An article is something

a written for an employer.

b written to find out information.

c written to a particular person.

d written to interest an unknown reader.

e written to tell a story.

f written in a very formal style.

2 Read the exam task, ignoring the article, then choose four of the suggested ideas in a–f below to include in your article. What order would you put them in?

You have seen this announcement in an entertainment magazine.

MY FAVOURITE ACTOR

Tell us about your favourite actor. We will publish the most interesting articles in our next issue of *Movie Mad* magazine.

Write your article in 120–180 words in an appropriate style.

a what roles they might play in the future

b a physical description of the actor

c a description of his or her private life

d some of the films he or she has appeared in

e why this particular actor is your favourite

f a description of the actor's character

3 Now read the article, ignoring the words in 1–8, and find out which of the suggested ideas in 2 the writer has included.

My favourite actor

I want to tell you about my favourite actor, Johnny Depp. [1]*Although / However / If* he is in his 40s, he is handsome, charming and physically very fit. [2]*While / In addition / Nevertheless*, he has a reputation for being a very good actor and working hard on the film set.

Johnny dropped out of school aged 15 to become a rock musician. But after being introduced to actor Nicholas Cage, he decided to turn his attention to acting. [3]*Later / After / Soon* appearing in *Edward Scissorhands*, he became a well-known star. [4]*Since / After / During* then, he has played many different parts in all kinds of films. He is now one of the most recognisable actors in the world.

Johnny Depp has acted in more than thirty feature films [5]*but / as / and* he has appeared in some of the most successful films in cinema history, including the *Pirates of the Caribbean* trilogy. Recent big box-office successes include films like *The Rum Diary* and *Public Enemies*.

So why do I like Johnny Depp? Well, I like him [6]*in order that / while / because* he seems to be an interesting and approachable kind of man [7]*despite / in spite / even if* his very successful acting career. Some film actors think that they are very important people, [8]*and / but / so* not Johnny Depp, who lives a quiet life in France for most of the year with French actress and singer, Vanessa Paradis. He considers himself to be a lucky man who just happens be a film star.

LINKING IDEAS

4 Match a–g with words which mean the same in 1–6. Which word in 1–6 matches with two words in a–g?

a although	1 during the time when
b in order to	2 even though
c because	3 since
d in addition	4 however
e nevertheless	5 so that
f while	6 moreover
g from that time	

5 Use words in 4 to complete sentences a–f. More than one answer may be possible.

a The film is quite old. _____, it is exciting in parts.

b We came to England _____ improve our English.

c _____ we were watching the DVD, the TV screen suddenly went blank.

d This actor has appeared in many films. _____, he has done a lot of work in the theatre.

e I like James Bond films _____ they have terrific stunts.

f _____ I don't watch much TV, I do enjoy watching soap operas.

6 Read the article again and choose the best link words for 1–8.

DESPITE, IN SPITE OF, ALTHOUGH

7 Complete sentences a–e using *despite, in spite,* or *although*.

a _____ the play was long, it was very interesting.

b _____ the length of the queue for the disco, we didn't have to wait too long to get in.

c I enjoy living in England, _____ of the awful weather!

d _____ there were some big names in the musical, the story was boring.

e Jake managed to get the job _____ not having the right qualifications.

WORDS CONNECTED WITH THE CINEMA

8 Use these words to complete sentences a–h.

new releases	screen	background music
acting	trailer	starring
special effects	leading role	

a If you watch the _____, you have some idea about whether you want to see the film or not.

b I don't watch many films on TV because I prefer to watch them on a big _____.

c The _____ can help to create a romantic atmosphere in a film.

d Sometimes the _____ of the main film stars is not as good as that of the minor characters.

e A star in a _____ can make millions of dollars.

f I remember seeing an enjoyable romantic comedy _____ Adam Sandler.

g I never go out and watch _____ at the cinema – I wait until the film comes out on DVD.

h Even if the acting isn't very good, it's worth seeing some films just for the amazing _____.

WRITING AN ARTICLE

9 Using the ideas and vocabulary in this section, write an article of 120–180 words describing your favourite actor and saying why you like him or her.

> ### » EXAM HELPLINE
>
> **Part 2: Article**
>
> » Read the question carefully, note your ideas and put them in order.
>
> » Use three or four paragraphs.
>
> » Use a neutral style and join your ideas with suitable link words.
>
> » Use the *Writing guide* on page 118.

WORD FORMATION

1 Discuss the questions.

  a How difficult do you think it is to learn to play a musical instrument?

  b If you could play a musical instrument really well, which one would you choose to play? Why?

2 Read the text below, ignoring the gaps, and find out what the writer and his friends did.

3 Read the text again. Use the word given in capitals at the end of some of the lines to form a word that fits in the gap in the same line.

» EXAM HELPLINE

Part 3: Word formation

» Read the text once quickly for overall meaning.

» Read it again sentence by sentence to identify the part of speech needed.

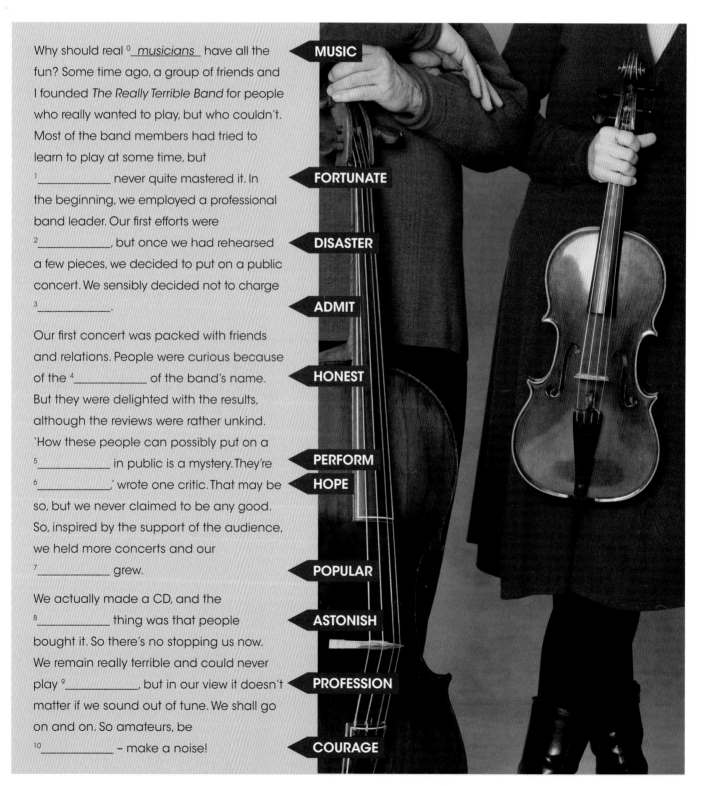

Why should real ⁰ _musicians_ have all the fun? Some time ago, a group of friends and I founded *The Really Terrible Band* for people who really wanted to play, but who couldn't. Most of the band members had tried to learn to play at some time, but ¹_____ never quite mastered it. In the beginning, we employed a professional band leader. Our first efforts were ²_____, but once we had rehearsed a few pieces, we decided to put on a public concert. We sensibly decided not to charge ³_____.

  MUSIC

  FORTUNATE

  DISASTER

  ADMIT

Our first concert was packed with friends and relations. People were curious because of the ⁴_____ of the band's name. But they were delighted with the results, although the reviews were rather unkind. 'How these people can possibly put on a ⁵_____ in public is a mystery. They're ⁶_____,' wrote one critic. That may be so, but we never claimed to be any good. So, inspired by the support of the audience, we held more concerts and our ⁷_____ grew.

  HONEST

  PERFORM

  HOPE

  POPULAR

We actually made a CD, and the ⁸_____ thing was that people bought it. So there's no stopping us now. We remain really terrible and could never play ⁹_____, but in our view it doesn't matter if we sound out of tune. We shall go on and on. So amateurs, be ¹⁰_____ – make a noise!

  ASTONISH

  PROFESSION

  COURAGE

NOUN ENDINGS: VERBS TO NOUNS

4 Make verbs a–h into nouns using these endings. You may need to change or add letters to the verbs. One of the words can be made into two nouns.

-er	-cion	-edge	-ance	-ion
-al	-ition	-sion	-ing	

Verb	Noun
a tolerate	_____
b include	_____
c meet	_____
d compose	_____
e know	_____
f suspect	_____
g rehearse	_____
h complete	_____

TEST YOUR KNOWLEDGE: PAST TENSES

Correct any mistakes you find in sentences a–e.

a Suddenly, the skies become dark and the wind started howling.

b I was performing in the band when I was seeing someone I knew.

c What did you do when you visited London?

d Who was this article wrote by?

e I was working as an engineer and my wife was writing a book.

PAST SIMPLE AND PAST CONTINUOUS

5 Match the uses of the past simple and the past continuous a–f with sentences 1–6.

a a series of actions in the past

b a regular past occurrence which no longer happens

c a past situation that existed over a certain period of time

d two actions happening together in the past

e a single action in the past

f an action going on when another action happened.

1 I didn't have much money when I was a student.

2 I got off the train in Manchester.

3 I used to go to a concert every week.

4 I got up early, had breakfast and caught the train into town.

5 I was driving to work when I heard the news.

6 We were sitting on a park bench and the children were playing nearby.

6 Put the verbs in brackets in sentences a–e into the correct form of the past simple or past continuous.

a I _____ (drive) to the airport when I _____ (realise) I had forgotten my passport.

b While I _____ (walk) through town the other day, I _____ (find) a really unusual bookshop.

c Mum _____ (make) dinner and dad _____ (lay) the table when someone _____ (ring) the doorbell.

d The whole family _____ (watch) TV when a news flash _____ (interrupt) the programme.

e Penny _____ (study) in Paris when she _____ (met) someone who _____ (change) her life completely.

PAST SIMPLE OR PAST CONTINUOUS PASSIVE?

7 Rewrite sentences a–c using the words given.

a They handed the tourists their tickets.

The tickets _____.

The tourists _____.

b They were giving the audience free drinks.

Free drinks _____.

The audience _____.

c They gave the fans autographed photos of the pop singer.

The fans _____.

Autographed _____.

USED TO (DO), WOULD (DO)

8 In which sentence can either used to or would be used? Why can only used to be used in the other sentence?

a Every winter, we _____ go to the mountains.

b This building _____ be an old palace.

9 Use these verbs and either used to or would to complete sentences a–e. More than one answer may be possible. In which sentences can't you use would?

be	take	like	live	give

a My grandparents _____ in Australia.

b Dad _____ us to the cinema on Saturdays when I was a child.

c You never _____ coffee!

d The teacher _____ us our homework on a Friday afternoon.

e There are far more cars on the roads than there _____.

MULTIPLE MATCHING

1 (⊙ 4) **Listen to some sentences and write words which mean the same as those in a–j.**

a can't bear

b didn't object

c amazing

d delayed

e interested in

f angry

g something unexpected that gives pleasure

h understand

i someone who is mad about something

j succeeded in doing something

> ### » EXAM HELPLINE
>
> **Part 3: Multiple matching**
>
> » Read the task carefully to get an idea of what the speakers will talk about.
>
> » Use the second listening to check that you do not need the option you have not used.

2 (⊙ 5) **You will hear five different people talking about events they went to recently. Choose from the list (A–F) how each person felt about the event. There is one extra letter which you do not need to use.**

A It was much too crowded to be enjoyable.

B Standing around wasn't very comfortable.

C It was much more fun than I'd expected.

D It was worth all the money I paid for the ticket.

E It wasn't the sort of thing I could enjoy.

F It wasn't as professional as I'd hoped.

Speaker 1	
Speaker 2	
Speaker 3	
Speaker 4	
Speaker 5	

> Do you enjoy the types of events the speakers went to? Why?/Why not?
>
> What's your idea of a really good night out?

03 SPEAKING

COLLABORATIVE TASK AND DISCUSSION

1 Put a tick next to each of the activities you would expect to do in Part 3 of the exam.

a turn-take

b invite your partner to speak

c start a conversation

d express your own opinion

e give personal information

f reply to your partner's questions

g ask the examiner questions

h agree or disagree

i make a suggestion

j reach a decision

2 Look at pictures 1–7, then read the exam task on page 106 and write down the following information. (Points c and d will appear above the pictures in the exam.)

a Length of task: _____

b What the pictures show: _____

c What to talk about: _____

d What to decide: _____

» EXAM HELPLINE

Part 3: Collaborative task

» Each Part 3 task has two parts: the first is talking about the visuals and the second is making a decision. Talk about all the visuals before making a decision.

» If you forget what to do, look at the questions above the pictures to remind yourself.

» Remember to talk about all the visuals before you make a decision.

3 With a partner, do the exam task in 2. Time yourselves for three minutes and see if you can talk about each picture and come to a decision in the time allowed. Use some of the phrases below, or others of your own.

Starting a conversation

So shall we begin with this one?

So let's start, shall we?

Right. I think we could start with this picture.

Inviting your partner to speak

What do you think?

What's your opinion?

What about you?

4 ⊙ 6 What happens in Part 4 of the exam? Listen to the recording, which is also on page 107.

1 Why is the first candidate's answer not a good one?

2 Why is the second candidate's answer a good one?

> Do you think it's possible to be happy all the time?
> Do you think it's better to be part of a large or a small family?
> How important do you think it is to have a lot of interests and hobbies?
> How long do you think school/work holidays should be?

COMPOUND ADJECTIVES Extension p26 ex3

1 Use these compound adjectives to complete sentences a–g.

second-hand	fair-skinned	home-made
hard-working	left-handed	well-known
kind-hearted		

a Kevin is a _____ student. He's also brilliant at maths.

b _____ people should use plenty of sun cream when they lie on the beach.

c It's a _____ fact that the more you earn, the more you spend.

d The shop sells things like scissors made specially for _____ people.

e I can't afford a new car so I'm going to buy a _____ one.

f Paula is such a _____ person – she's always buying people presents.

g This _____ soup is much better than anything from a supermarket.

EXPRESSIONS WITH *KICK* Revision p26 ex5

2 Use an expression with *kick* to complete sentences a–d.

a What time does the match _____ tomorrow afternoon?

b Why did James get _____ of the rugby club? Did he do something awful?

c I hate people who _____ about something in a public place – it's so embarrassing.

d Honestly, I could _____ for refusing the invitation to the party – apparently it was fantastic.

3 Complete sentences a–c so that they are true for you.

a I would kick up a fuss if _____.

b I could kick myself for _____.

c I would hate to be kicked out of _____.

ADJECTIVES ENDING IN *-ED* AND *-ING*

Extension p27 text

4 Form the appropriate adjective ending in *-ed* or *-ing* from these verbs to complete sentences a–f. More than one answer may be possible.

distress	excite	bore	terrify
amaze	embarrass	amuse	

a I'm always _____ when I watch horror films.

b When I saw the film, I was _____ by the special effects.

c Films about wars are always _____ because lots of people die in them.

d I always feel _____ if I start to cry at the cinema.

e Some romantic comedies are _____, but others are just _____.

f I wonder why people find disaster movies so _____. I can't stand them!

WORDS CONNECTED WITH THE CINEMA

Revision p29 ex8

5 Write words connected with the cinema to match the meanings a–h.

a what you hear playing as you watch a film

  b _ _ _ _ _ _ _ _ _   m _ _ _ _

b what performers are doing in a film

  a _ _ _ _ _

c being the most important actors in a film

  s _ _ _ _ _ _ _

d films which have only just come out

  n _ _   r _ _ _ _ _ _ _

e what you watch a film on at the cinema

  s _ _ _ _ _

f a short extract from a film about to be released

  t _ _ _ _ _ _

g the main acting part in a film

  l _ _ _ _ _ _   r _ _ _

h what can make watching a film amazing or interesting

  s _ _ _ _ _ _   e _ _ _ _ _ _

WRITING Extension p28–29

6 Write a paragraph (about 150 words) describing a good film that you remember well. Say

 – when you first saw it.

 – who you saw it with.

 – why you liked it.

 – how it is different from other films you have seen.

DESPITE, IN SPITE OF, ALTHOUGH

Revision p29 ex7

7 Use *despite, in spite* or *although* and the information in a–f to write beginnings for the sentence endings 1–6.

Example: *Despite feeling unwell, Paul still went to work.*

a _____ feeling unwell

b _____ I had no money

c _____ of the warm weather

d _____ the long journey

e _____ we had been waiting for over an hour

f _____ of the rain

1 Paul still went to work.

2 we arrived at our destination feeling enthusiastic.

3 the children were playing football in the park.

4 I was happy.

5 everyone in the queue was cheerful.

6 the inside of the house was freezing cold.

NOUN ENDINGS: VERBS TO NOUNS

Extension p31 ex4

8 Make nouns from the verbs in a–j using these endings. You may have to make other changes. Which two verbs can you use to make two nouns each?

-er	-cion	-sion	-ition
-edge	-al	-ance	-ing

verbs	nouns
a assist	_____
b refuse	_____
c suspect	_____
d decide	_____
e paint	_____
f know	_____
g compete	_____
h deny	_____
i revise	_____
j cook	_____

PAST SIMPLE, PAST CONTINUOUS, OR *USED TO?* Revision p31 ex5–9

9 Complete the text with the correct form of the verbs in brackets.

Every summer when the children were small, we
[1]_____ (go) to the South of France on holiday. We
always [2]_____ (take) the car on these trips. One
summer, while we [3]_____ (travel) along a particularly
beautiful stretch of road on our return journey, my
husband, who [4]_____ (do) the map reading at the
time, [5]_____ (decide) to take a detour. The children
always [6]_____ (listen) to music in the back of the car
on these long journeys, but by this time, they [7]_____
(get bored) and [8]_____ (need) something else to
entertain them. As I [9]_____ (drive) round one of the
sharp bends, I suddenly [10]_____ (notice) that the
road [11]_____ (become) narrower and narrower. After
about 20 minutes, it suddenly [12]_____ (come) to an
abrupt end. It [13] _____ (begin) to look as if we might
get more excitement than we had expected that night!

MULTIPLE CHOICE

1 **Can you name these objects? What do you think they might have in common?**

2 **Read the extract from a short story and choose the best title.**

   a The House in the Valley

   b A Treasured Possession

   c A Life of Poverty

> Do you own any special objects? Why are they special? How would you feel if you lost them?

3 **Read the story again. For questions 1–8, choose the answer (A, B, C or D) which you think fits best according to the text.**

   1 How did Jack get his medal?

     A He was given it shortly after he was born.

     B His mother gave it to him when he was eleven.

     C His aunt gave one to all Mrs Digby's children.

     D A relative gave it to him because she liked it.

   2 What does the writer mean by 'could have done with' in line 12?

     A would have been better off with

     B would have had no connection with

     C would have got rid of

     D would have taken an interest in

   3 Mrs Piercy advised Jack to

     A look after the medal in case of hard times ahead.

     B take the medal with him wherever he went.

     C hide the medal from the younger family members.

     D treasure the medal as his own personal possession.

   4 Why did Jack take the hill path one day?

     A He wanted to see the big house at Watching.

     B He had not been able to get a lift to a nearby village.

     C He decided to go for a short walk to Hending.

     D He thought he must have lost his medal there.

1   Jack Digby's mother never gave him anything. Perhaps, as a poor woman, she had nothing to give, or perhaps she was not sure how to divide anything between the nine children. His aunt, Mrs Piercy the

5   poulterer's wife, did give him something, a keepsake in the form of a medal. The date on it was September the 12th, 1663, which happened to be Jack's birthday, although by the time she gave it to him he was eleven years old. On the back there was the figure of an

10   angel and a motto, *Desideratus* (something needed or wished for), which perhaps didn't fit the case too well, since Mrs Digby could have done with fewer, rather than more, children. However, it had taken Mrs Piercy's fancy.

15   Jack thanked her, and she advised him to stow it away safely, out of reach of the other children. Jack was amazed that she should think anywhere was out of reach of his little sisters. 'You should have had it earlier,' said Mrs Piercy, 'but those were hard times.' Jack told

20   her that he was very glad to have something of which he could say, 'This is my own,' and she answered, though not with much conviction, that he mustn't set too much importance on earthly possessions.

    He kept the medal with him always, only

25   transferring it, as the year went by, from his summer to his winter breeches. But anything you carry about with you in your pocket you are bound to lose sooner or later. Jack had an errand to do in Hending, but there was nothing on the road that day, neither horse nor

30   cart, no hope of cadging a lift, so after waiting for an hour or so he began to walk over by the hill path.

    After about a mile the hill slopes away sharply towards Watching, which is not a village and never was, only a great house standing among its outbuildings

⁴⁰ almost at the bottom of the valley. Jack stopped there for a while to look down at the smoke from the chimneys and to calculate, as anyone might have done, the number of dinners that were being cooked there that day. If he dropped or lost his keepsake he did not know it at the ⁴⁵ time, for as is commonly the case he didn't miss it until he reached home again. Then he went through his pockets, but the shining medal was gone and he could only repeat, 'I had it when I started out.'

The winter frosts began and one day Jack thought, 'I ⁵⁰ had better try going that way again.' He halted, as before, to look at the great house, and then at the ice under his feet, for all the streams and ponds were frozen on every side of him, all hard as a bone. In a little hole just to the left of the path, something no bigger than a small ⁵⁵ puddle, but deep, he saw, through the transparency of the ice, the keepsake he had been given. He had nothing in his hand to break the ice. 'Well then, jump on it.' But that got him nowhere. 'I'll wait until the ice has gone,' he thought. 'The season is turning, we'll get a thaw in a ⁶⁰ day or two.'

On the next Sunday, he was up there again, and made straight for the little hole, and found nothing. It was empty, after that short time, of ice and even of water. And because the idea of recovering the keepsake had ⁶⁵ occupied his whole mind that day, the disappointment made him feel lost, like a stranger to the country. Then he noticed that there was an earthenware pipe laid straight down the side of the hill, and that this must very likely have carried off the water from his hole, and ⁷⁰ everything in it. No mystery as to where it led. 'The stable-yards,' thought Jack. His Desideratus had been washed down there, he was as sure of that now as if he'd seen it go.

5 What happened to Jack one frosty winter's day?
   A He discovered his medal in a small pool of water.
   B He found the medal he had lost.
   C He found a keepsake similar to his own in the ice.
   D He broke his hand on the ice in a pool of water.

6 What did Jack realise the following Sunday?
   A Someone must have found his medal in the hole and kept it.
   B Someone had picked up his medal and thrown it down the hill.
   C His medal had been hidden under an earthenware pipe.
   D His medal had probably been washed away down the hill.

7 What does 'it' refer to in line 70?
   A the hill path
   B the hole
   C the earthenware pipe
   D the water

8 What do we learn about Jack's attitude towards his medal in the extract?
   A He was rather disappointed with it.
   B He suspected that one day he would lose it.
   C He knew he would not receive anything like it again.
   D He was determined to find his lost treasure.

CONFUSING WORDS

4 **Some of these words are in the text. Use each pair of words to complete sentences a–h.**

advise/warn

a What would you _____ me to study for the exam?

b Did Mary _____ the children not to skate on the thin ice?

reach/arrive

c When you _____ at the crossroads, turn left.

d If you hurry, you will _____ the town before dark.

miss/lose

e Whenever I wear gloves, I always seem to _____ one.

f If I left home, I know I would _____ my family.

drop/fall

g Please don't _____ that vase – it's worth a fortune!

h Sammy didn't _____ off the chair – his sister pushed him.

REPORT

1 Which of features a–h do you think you might find in a report?

a informal language

b three-paragraph layout

c topic headings

d suggestions and recommendations

e contractions

f each new idea in a separate section

g numbered points

h facts and figures

2 Read the exam question and complete the mind map below with your ideas.

Some English-speaking students are coming to stay with families in your town on a week's exchange trip. The organisers have asked you to write a report suggesting what activities they might do during their stay. Include information on different kinds of activities and how popular they might be with students.

Write your report in 120–180 words.

Here are four activities which I consider to be suitable for the students coming to stay in my town, Bristol.

A _____

What students need is some information about our citys' history and what happened here in the past. We are lucky to have lots of historical buildings, a famous bridge and even a historical ship in the area, and I ¹_____ the students to one or two of these during their stay.

B _____

On the outskirts of Bristol there is a zoo. The students ²_____ a guided tour of the zoo and learn about the animals which you can find there.

3 Read the report above about a city called Bristol, ignoring the gaps and any mistakes. Were any of the ideas similar to yours?

What activities to include? Why?

Surrounding area is beautiful and you can have a picnic there or in one of the many parks nearby.

C _____

I ³_____ to the new sports centre. The students will find all kinds of sports there and can enjoy the open-air swimming pool if the weather will be fine.

D _____

Finally, I ⁴_____ are taken to a restaurant to try some dishes which are characteristic of the area and which they may not have tried. These cultural and leisure activities should make the students' stay enjoyable.

4 Write suitable topic headings for paragraphs A–D.

5 There are three mistakes in the report. Can you find and correct them?

MAKING SUGGESTIONS AND RECOMMENDATIONS

6 Complete gaps 1–4 in the report using these phrases.

  a suggest that the students
  b could have
  c suggest taking
  d would definitely recommend going

7 You can make recommendations in a report using *should*, *I recommend* and *I suggest* and the passive. Rewrite sentences a–e using the words in brackets.

  Examples:

  Take the students to the local library. (should)
  The students should be taken to the local library.

  Show the students the port area. (recommend)
  I recommend that the students are shown the port area.

  Invite the students to a party. (suggest)
  I suggest that the students are invited to a party.

  a Show the students the new shopping centre. (should)
  b Give the students a free afternoon to explore the town. (recommend)
  c Introduce the students to some local people. (suggest)
  d Take the students on a river cruise. (recommend)
  e Encourage the students to learn more about our local history. (should)

EMPHASISING A POINT

8 You can emphasise something by using *What* at the beginning of the sentence and the verb *to be*. Rewrite sentences a–d as in the example.

  Example:

  Students need to get to know the area.
  What students need is to get to know the area.

  a Students really want somewhere to meet.
  b We mustn't forget that students don't like being on their own.
  c It's important that the exchange trip is a success.
  d We should remember that it is impossible to please everybody.

WRITING A REPORT

9 Write a report for the organisers like the one about Bristol, but referring to the area where you live. Use the mind map in 2 and expressions from 6–8.

> **» EXAM HELPLINE**
>
> **Part 2: Report**
> » A mind map can help with ideas and planning.
> » Include all the information asked for.
> » Use headings for each new paragraph in a report.
> » Use a neutral style.
> » Use the *Writing guide* on page 119.

TEST YOUR KNOWLEDGE: THE FUTURE

Match the future forms in sentences a–i with uses 1–9.

a I'm going to stay in and read a good book tonight.

b The earth's resources will run out in 50 years' time.

c I'm having a job interview on Thursday.

d I'll buy you an ice cream when we get to the park.

e I will pass my driving test no matter how many times I have to take it!

f The forecast says it's going to be a nice day tomorrow.

g I'll have finished this homework by lunchtime.

h Shall I do the washing-up this evening?

i What will we all be doing ten years from now?

1 talking about an action which will be taking place at a certain future time

2 saying something is probable, based on evidence

3 making a promise

4 making an offer

5 making a firm prediction

6 talking about an action which will be finished before a certain future time

7 expressing an intention

8 expressing determination

9 talking about a definite future arrangement

1 Make sentences of your own using suitable future forms and the ideas in a–i.

a Promise to send someone a postcard.

b Say what you intend to do this weekend.

c Offer to help tidy up someone's room.

d Make a prediction about the world's wildlife.

e Say what you think the black clouds in the sky mean.

f Describe an arrangement you have made for tomorrow.

g Say what you are determined to do in the near future.

h Say when you'll have finished doing something.

i Say where you'll be spending your holidays next summer.

FUTURE CONTINUOUS OR FUTURE PERFECT?

2 Complete sentences a–h using the future continuous (*will be doing*) or the future perfect (*will have done*).

a This time next week we _____ (lie) on a beach in Spain.

b We _____ (finished) this unit by the end of the week.

c My friend Lucy _____ (come) on holiday with us this summer.

d By the end of this course I _____ (write) ten compositions.

e Do you think you _____ (visit) Australia when you go on your round-the-world trip?

f I hope I _____ (pass) my exam by this time next year.

g By the year 2050, the world's population _____ (increase) dramatically.

h This time next month, we _____ (drive) across Europe on our way to Greece.

3 Look at the time lines below and write four sentences saying what you think Tim and Dave *will be doing* or *will have done* at the different times.

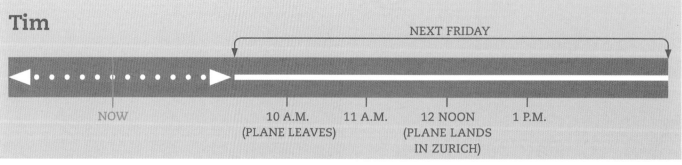

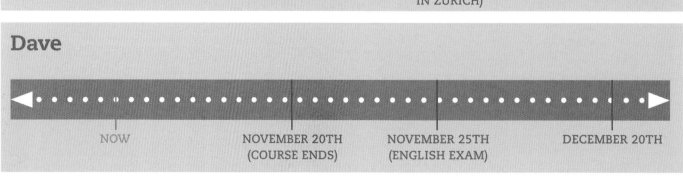

OTHER WAYS OF TALKING ABOUT THE FUTURE

4 *Be due to (do), be on the point of (doing)* and *be about to (do)* are used to talk about future events. Which two mean the same thing? Match the expression(s) to meanings a–b.

  a everyone expects something to happen, e.g. like an event on a timetable

  b *be ready* to do something

5 Use the correct form of the expressions in 4 to complete sentences a–f. More than one answer may be possible.

  a We _____ leaving the house when we realised we had lost our keys.

  b The plane _____ take off at 2.30, but it was delayed by half an hour.

  c I _____ leave for the airport. Can I phone you when I get back?

  d The new motorway _____ be finished next year.

  e I _____ giving up my job and starting to look for something more challenging.

  f When _____ the schools _____ break up for the summer holidays?

KEY WORD TRANSFORMATIONS

> **EXAM HELPLINE**

Part 4: Key word transformations

» Think carefully about the meaning of the first sentence. Identify any key structures.

» Don't change the key word.

» The key word may not be the part of speech you first think of.

» Items which are often tested include:
  - tense changes
  - phrasal verbs
  - the passive
  - lexical phrases
  - modals

6 For questions 1–8, complete the second sentence so that it has a similar meaning to the first sentence, using the word given. Do not change the word given. You must use between two and five words, including the word given.

Example:

  0 Our local festival is due to be held in March this year.

  take

  Our local festival *will take place* in March this year.

  1 On Monday I'm going to give the teacher my report about facilities in our town.

  handed

  By Tuesday, I _____ the teacher my report about facilities in our town.

  2 This seaside town is not an important port nowadays.

  used

  This seaside town _____ an important port.

  3 A new baby clinic is urgently needed in the area.

  need

  We are _____ a new baby clinic in the area.

  4 It will be impossible to reach the village if it snows.

  off

  The village _____ if it snows.

  5 There is too little green space in this city.

  not

  There _____ green space in this city.

  6 Years ago, there was no other public transport besides trams in our city.

  form

  Years ago, trams were _____ public transport in our city.

  7 What attracts you to this part of the world?

  find

  What _____ this part of the world?

  8 I'm excited about having an English-speaking student to stay with us.

  looking

  I _____ having an English-speaking student to stay with us.

MULTIPLE CHOICE

1 Discuss the questions.

a What kind of homes do you think people will live in in the future?

b How do you think our working lives will change in the future?

2 Read the questions. What do you think the people will be talking about in the recording?

1 How does Jim see family life in the future?

A People will have much more time to enjoy themselves.

B Spending time with family members will be more difficult.

C People will spend more time looking after their families.

2 Why does Jim think many people will change their way of working?

A There will be fewer jobs available.

B Commuting damages the environment.

C Fuel supplies will eventually run out.

3 What does Jim suggest companies might do in the future?

A Control their employees by means of technology.

B Create giant conference centres around the world.

C Make sure their employees communicate only with them.

4 How does Jim see patterns of work changing?

A Working hours will be much more fixed than they are now.

B Workers will be able to work the hours that suit them.

C Workers won't have any choice about the hours that they work.

5 How does Jim think young people will be affected by future changes?

A They will be much more willing to do any kind of work.

B They will want to do jobs that are more meaningful.

C They will have less responsibility than the older generation.

6 What does Jim say might happen to people with exceptional abilities?

A They will earn more.

B They will work less.

C They will retire earlier.

7 What final comment does Jim make about the future?

A We'll throw away twice as much as we do now.

B We won't be able to find household items easily.

C We'll start to make products that last longer.

≫ EXAM HELPLINE

Part 4: Multiple choice

≫ Read the questions and try to predict what you are going to hear.

≫ You will hear the recording twice.

3 ⊙ 7 You will hear an interview with Jim Benson, a sociologist who is talking about what he thinks life will be like for ordinary people in the future. For questions 1–7, choose the best answer (A, B or C).

Which of Jim's predictions do you think might come true?

If you could make one prediction about the future, what would it be?

04 SPEAKING

THE LONG TURN

1 Which words can be used to describe what the people are doing in the photos in tasks 1 and 2?

queuing	fresh air	shower
stadium	barriers	heatwave
indoors	scarf	outside
umbrella	picnic	supporters

2 In pairs, choose one pair of photos each, then do the exam tasks in turn. Answer the question when your partner has finished speaking.

Task 1 *Student A*

Compare these photos and say how the weather is affecting what the people are doing.

Question for Student B

What kind of weather do you enjoy most?

Task 2 *Student B*

Compare these photos and say why you think the people are having to stand in a queue.

Question for Student A

What kinds of things do you have to queue for?

» EXAM HELPLINE

Part 2: The long turn

» Each pair of photos and tasks will be completely different.

» If you finish too quickly, give a personal reaction to the photos and the task.

» Don't wait too long before you start speaking.

3 Decide which suggestions a–e would improve your performance, and why the others are not a good idea.

a If you don't understand what you have to do, ask the examiner to repeat the task.

b If you can't think of anything to say, keep saying the same thing repeatedly.

c Ask the examiner how much time you have left.

d Relate the pictures to your own experience.

e If you can't remember how to say something in English, ask the examiner what the word is.

EXPRESSIONS WITH DO Extension p 36/37 text

1 Underline the expressions with *do* in sentences a–d and match them with meanings 1–4.

a We'll have to do without a holiday this year. We just can't afford one.

b A person's intelligence has nothing to do with how hard they work.

c In many countries they have done away with the monarchy.

d It was a tiring journey, and we could have done with more breaks.

1 end

2 has no connection with

3 need

4 manage without having

2 Use the correct form of the expressions in 1 to complete sentences a–d.

a I'm sure the robbery had _____ the new neighbours who moved in last week.

b After waiting almost an hour for a bus, I could have _____ a cup of coffee.

c It's easy to travel in most European countries because they have _____ border checks.

d There's no milk in the fridge, so you'll just have to _____ it!

ADJECTIVES EXPRESSING FEELINGS
Extension p36/37 text

3 Divide these adjectives into three groups.

a positive   b negative   c positive or negative

amazed	disappointed	glad	upset
surprised	angry	delighted	bored
impatient	curious	amused	excited

4 Match adjectives in 3 to the situations a–e which might make you experience them. More than one answer may be possible.

a winning a competition

b studying a subject that you aren't interested in

c hearing some important news and wanting to find out exactly what happened

d having an argument with a friend

e looking forward to a special treat

PHRASAL VERBS WITH GO
Extension p36/37 text

5 Match meanings a–f with the phrasal verbs in sentences 1–6.

a examine or discuss something carefully

b become bad

c pass

d become ill

e be keen on

f continue

1 Time *goes by* more quickly as you get older.

2 Let's *go over* the most important grammar points again.

3 Please *go on* with what you were saying.

4 I like some classical music, but I don't *go in for* opera.

5 I think this milk has *gone off*!

6 Sam has *gone down with* a bad cold.

BOUND TO, LIKELY TO Extension p36/37 text

6 Match these phrases with the explanations a–b.

likely to	bound to

a This means that something is certain to happen.

b This means that there is a very good chance that something will happen.

7 Use *bound* or *likely* to complete sentences a–e.

a It's _____ to rain if we go for a walk. It always does.

b Pat's _____ to pass the exam. She's really clever and she's studied so hard.

c Ted's quite _____ to visit us this weekend, isn't he?

d They say our team will win the next World Cup, but I don't think it's very _____ to, do you?

e William's _____ to be on time. He's never late.

HAD BETTER (NOT) Extension p36/37 text

8 What does *I'd better try going that way again* from paragraph 5 in the text mean? Choose the correct meaning (a or b) then make sentences using *had better (not)* to give advice in situations 1–5.

a I would like to go that way again.

b It would be a good idea to go that way again.

1 I don't feel well.

2 I forgot to tell my parents that I would be late.

3 My friend Jim wants to travel round the world, but he hasn't got any money.

4 I can't swim.

5 I'm allergic to tomatoes.

WRITING Extension p 36/37 text

9 You have lost something which means a lot to you. Write a notice to put on a noticeboard saying

- what you have lost.
- where and when you think you might have lost it.
- why it is important to you.

THE FUTURE Revision p40 ex1–3

10 Choose the correct form of the verb (a, b, c or d) to complete 1–6 below.

1. a will have met   b is meeting
   c will be met   d will have been met
2. a will set   b will have set
   c will have been set   d will be set
3. a are going to   b will
   c will be   d will have been
4. a are carrying   b will have carried
   c will be carrying   d will be carried
5. a is going to design   b is designing
   c will design   d will have been designed
6. a is being   b will be being
   c will have been   d will be

Tomorrow, the government body charged with city planning ¹...... with construction companies. In the course of their discussions, they ²...... a target of constructing two million more homes in the south-east of England by 2020. If we ³...... build even more houses for people living in larger towns and cities, we need to make that accommodation both affordable and more environmentally friendly. Over the next few years, the government ⁴...... out more research into new, energy-saving technologies for homes. It is hoped that within ten years, far more efficient heating systems ⁵...... and ⁶...... ready to install in some of the new homes under construction.

OTHER WAYS OF TALKING ABOUT THE FUTURE Revision p41 ex4–5

11 Rewrite the words in italics in sentences a–i using the words in brackets. You may have to change the order of the words in the sentence.

a We *were going to go* for a walk, but it started to rain. (about)

b I *was going to lock* the door when the phone rang. (point)

c We *are expecting* the train *to arrive* any minute now. (due)

d Tim *was going to tell* me his big secret when someone came into the room. (about)

e The president is *going to give* a speech at the World Environmental Conference next month. (due)

f Our neighbours *were going to move*, but they changed their minds. (point)

g Anya *was going to explain* what happened when we were cut off. (about)

h My aunt *was going to go* into hospital for an operation, but it was cancelled at the last minute. (about)

i We *thought* our guests *would come* last night, but they arrived this morning. (due)

05 READING

MISSING SENTENCES

1 Read the article, ignoring the gaps. What natural disaster had recently occurred when the writer visited the islands? Who is Arthur?

Escape from Paradise

We arrived at the Cayman Islands shortly after Hurricane Michelle had swept by. Waiting for us was our host, who was taking us on a catamaran ride to visit Suzie, Daisy and their friends. These improbably-
5 named females are stingrays and they can be found about four miles from the coast of Grand Cayman in an area called Stingray City. It's a ridiculously inappropriate name because 'city' creates images of traffic jams and skyscrapers, whereas this is a quiet
10 corner of the Caribbean Sea, very near the reef. **1** ☐ Bear in mind that Seven Mile Beach is so called because it's five and a half miles long! Against that background, it soon becomes pretty clear that it's best not to take things at their face value.
15 We stopped at Stingray Bar where you can stand waist-deep in the warm water and play footsie with these gentle, peace-loving creatures which don't sting (that's another misnomer). However, their sharp tails will give you a nasty cut if you kick them.
20 Quite right, too! **2** ☐ The one I held felt rather like an oversized Portobello mushroom.
The stingrays did not seem to be any the worse for wear after Hurricane Michelle's passage. Nor did the 303 aquatic creatures we had the privilege of
25 meeting on the first Friday of November. **3** ☐ The event is financed by an organisation which was originally set up in the late 1960s. It is now the largest project of its kind in the world.
In order to study their behaviour in their natural
30 habitat, each year the organisation tags and releases from its farm about 1,000 one-year-old green

turtles, some of which have been seen as far afield as Venezuela and the United States. Most of these are released privately, but each year residents and visitors
35 can join the fun and support the research initiative by sponsoring a turtle, (i.e. paying to release it into the wild). A minimum contribution of $15 – which can be paid over the internet before your visit – allows you to adopt one of these creatures. It also enables you to deposit
40 it in the shallow waters off the Safehaven beach. **4** ☐ Instead of living on the farm for the rest of their lives, they are instantly given licence to roam freely throughout the waters of the Caribbean.
5 ☐ Many of the youngsters we met at Safehaven had
45 formed emotional bonds with their chosen turtles. A small child told me he had named his turtle Chocolate and, apparently in sympathy, my partner named hers Milky Bar. Given the tendency of chocolate to be eaten, those names seemed to be tempting fate. I wanted something
50 that sounded more solid, so mine ended up with Arthur, although as I carried him to the sea, I'm not sure who was in a worse state of panic. **6** ☐
Eventually he swam away confidently and enthusiastically. Although the same could scarcely be
55 said for all the other 303 turtles, some of whom seemed totally confused by the entire episode. **7** ☐
Happily, in the end, all the turtles seemed to get the hang of it. We all stood watching as 303 heads bobbed up and down in the sunset, moving gradually out
60 to sea. As Arthur and his chums explored their new accommodation for the first time, we strolled back through the golf course at Safehaven to ours.

2 Seven sentences have been removed from the article. Choose from the sentences A–H the one which fits each gap (1–7). There is one extra sentence which you do not need to use.

A This was the Islands' annual turtle freedom day, an occasion that nobody should miss.

B He was palpitating furiously, while I was terrified of dropping the poor creature at a vital moment in his life.

C If you want to do the same, don't let the reputation for mixed weather put you off, for the islands are safe in most storms.

D Unsurprisingly, the turtle release is an especially popular event among children, for whom it is also an educational one.

E Not that this is unusual in the Cayman Islands.

F One paddled in a small and comical semi-circle on the beach's edge, soon returning to land after apparently having decided that he was not looking forward to the opportunity of exploring his new home.

G For the animals themselves, being picked is the equivalent of winning the lottery.

H Nevertheless, if you treat them with respect and (better still) if you feed them, they are quite happy to be held by visitors in search of unusual photo opportunities.

What do you think it would be like to spend a holiday in the Cayman Islands?
How important do you think animal conservation is?

USING ADVERBS

3 Make adverbs from these adjectives and find six of them in the text and missing sentences. Then use the adverbs to complete sentences a–h. Besides -ly, you may need to add other letters to the words.

scarce	special	furious
total	free	gradual
original	enthusiastic	

a After their release, the turtles were able to swim _____ in the open sea.

b What you are saying is _____ untrue!

c All the children shouted _____ that they would love to learn how to scuba dive.

d Pat's dog swam _____ against the strong current.

e This building was _____ an old boat house.

f These shoes were _____ made for me in Italy.

g We have _____ any money left for holidays this year.

h The turtles _____ made their way down to the sea, but it was a long, slow process.

VERBS OF MOVEMENT

4 Match these verbs from the article with meanings a–e, then use them in the correct form to complete sentences 1–5.

sweep	roam	paddle
bob	stroll	

a move up and down quickly

b move or push with force

c walk around an area in no particular direction

d walk in a leisurely way

e move or swim in shallow water

1 In this part of the safari park, animals are allowed to _____ around wherever they like.

2 We could just make out the seal's head _____ above the waves.

3 After its owner had thrown a stick into the pond, the small dog _____ out to fetch it.

4 A huge wave hit the boat and _____ everyone on deck off their feet.

5 Jim and Barbara _____ to the water's edge and watched the sun setting over the sea.

ESSAY

1 Many people in the world live on small islands. What do you think are the good things about living on an island? What are the disadvantages?

2 Read the exam task and make a plan for the answer.

As part of a project comparing life on an island with life on the mainland, you have been asked to write an essay of 120–180 words giving your opinions about the following statement.

Why would anyone choose to leave an island and move to a mainland city?

ESSAY PLAN

Paragraph 1
Introduction saying _____
_____
_____
_____
_____

Paragraph 2
Mention points for moving to a mainland city
_____
_____
_____
_____

Paragraph 3
Mention points against moving to a mainland city
_____
_____
_____
_____

Paragraph 4
Summarise whether _____
_____
_____
_____

3 Read the essay, ignoring the gaps, and compare it to your plan in 2. How many points does the writer make for and against living on the mainland?

More and more young people in countries like Britain, Croatia and Greece are deserting the islands where they grew up and moving to big towns on the mainland in search of jobs and excitement. [1]_____ is life on the mainland as fantastic as some people make it out to be?

A mainland city has many advantages. [2]_____, everything you could possibly want is nearby. [3]_____, there is plenty of cheap and reliable public transport. [4]_____, there are far more job opportunities.

[5]_____, living on the mainland has its disadvantages. [6]_____, the heavy traffic means that there is a lot of pollution. [7]_____ that because there are far more people, it is easy to feel isolated and not feel a part of the community. [8]_____, the mainland is more dangerous than an island because more crime takes place there.

[9]_____, we can see that [10]_____ there may be advantages to living on the mainland, there are also many drawbacks.

4 Complete gaps 1–10 in the essay using a–j. More than one answer may be possible.

a to sum up
b on the other hand
c although
d first of all
e to begin with
f last but not least
g secondly
h so
i finally
j another point is

> The essay would get a good mark. Why?

WORDS WITH SIMILAR MEANINGS

5 Find words and phrases in the essay which mean the same as a–h.

a greater numbers of
b leaving
c wonderful
d claim it is
e close
f dependable
g lonely
h disadvantages

MAKING COMPARISONS

6 There are three examples of comparisons in the essay: *as … as*, *far more* and *more … than*. Make similar comparisons using the information in a–e and your own ideas. You may need to change the order of the words.

a cities/small villages
b people on islands/in mainland towns
c life in the countryside/city
d cost of accommodation on islands/the mainland
e entertainment on the mainland/islands

EXPRESSIONS WITH *FEEL*

7 *Feel isolated* and *feel a part of* appear in the essay. What do they mean? Match the expressions with *feel* in a–e with the definitions 1–5.

a *Feel free* to say exactly what you think.
b Do you *feel like* going to the cinema?
c Getting a good mark in my composition made me *feel good*.
d I don't *feel up to* going to school today.
e Does it *feel strange* to be back on this island after such a long time away?

1 would like to
2 seem unusual
3 be happy
4 be ready to face or deal with
5 don't hesitate

WRITING AN ESSAY

8 As part of the same project in 2, you have been asked to write an essay of 120–180 words giving your opinions about the following statement.

Why would anyone want to work in the countryside?

Write your essay using some of the ideas in this section.

> **» EXAM HELPLINE**
>
> **Part 2: Essay**
> » Present both points of view, giving your opinions in a formal or neutral way.
> » Remember you can agree or disagree with the statement.
> » Use the *Writing guide* on page 120.

05 USE OF ENGLISH

MULTIPLE-CHOICE CLOZE

1 Read the text quickly, ignoring the gaps. What did the Polynesians have to do when they arrived in New Zealand?

> How difficult do you think it will be for New Zealand's Maoris to keep their cultural identity? Why do you think so many tourists visit New Zealand?

2 For questions 1–12, read the text again and decide which answer (A, B, C or D) best fits each gap.

0	A reaching	B arriving	C coming	D entering
1	A crowded	B complete	C full	D plenty
2	A combination		B completion	
	C competition		D comparison	
3	A reason	B purpose	C matter	D cause
4	A speak	B tell	C talk	D say
5	A consideration		B conversation	
	C discussion		D debate	
6	A state	B manner	C case	D way
7	A special	B separate	C different	D unusual
8	A escape	B prevent	C avoid	D check
9	A inhabited	B existed	C lived	D lasted
10	A fear	B difficulty	C doubt	D problem
11	A feel	B make	C become	D get
12	A rests	B survives	C continues	D remains

LAND OF THE LONG WHITE CLOUD

Imagine you're a Polynesian settler ⁰_____ in New Zealand one thousand years ago. You find a land of majestic snow-capped peaks, glaciers, fjords and volcanoes. You discover tall forests of fern trees ¹_____ of strange birds. And incredibly, there are no people living there. You name the islands Aotearoa, which means 'Land of the long white cloud'.

New Zealand is a ²_____ of different climates and landscapes, stretching from the tropical beaches around the Bay of Islands to the cold fjords and high mountains in the South Island. And it's a long way from anywhere else. For this simple ³_____ New Zealand was the last large landmass to be colonised, apart from Antarctica. Anthropologists ⁴_____ the story of a remarkable migration as the Polynesian ancestors of the Maori people sailed through the Pacific, landing on the islands after a long voyage in open canoes. There is some ⁵_____ as to when this actually happened, but the date is around 1,000 AD. In any ⁶_____ , it is very recent in terms of human history.

The land was ⁷_____ from anything the Polynesians had seen anywhere else in the Pacific. On the South Island, it was cold enough to ⁸_____ the growth of traditional crops. So the Polynesians had to adapt to conditions they had never experienced before. Nevertheless, they lived well in their new land for over six hundred years until December 1642, when Dutch explorer Abel Tazman became the first European explorer to see New Zealand.

In all the time that New Zealand has been ⁹_____ , no period has seen such a dramatic change as the time since the arrival of the European settlers. The Maoris had to suddenly adapt to life in a European society. The last three hundred years have seen a lot of changes for the Maori people, and these changes will, no ¹⁰_____ , continue. The challenge for the Maori will be to ¹¹_____ sure that despite all the changes, their culture ¹²_____ distinctly different.

Correct the mistakes in sentences a–e.

a Have you ever gone to Spain?

b Ben's moved to France, isn't he?

c I've lived here since three years.

d Haven't you finished your homework still?

e I've been think about going to New Zealand for a while.

PRESENT PERFECT SIMPLE AND CONTINUOUS

3 **Match the verb forms in a–e with the uses 1–5.**

a You've torn your jacket!

b My parents have bought a house in Spain.

c I've been studying English for five years.

d This is the third time I've seen this film.

e I've been waiting for you for over an hour.

1 to show we are more interested in what has happened than when it happened

2 to emphasise how many times an action happened

3 to show that the action is finished but we can see the result

4 to emphasise the length of the action

5 to suggest that this is still true or happening

4 **Complete sentences a–f using the present perfect simple or continuous.**

a I _____(stay) with my sister for the past few months.

b I _____ (live) in three different countries.

c This is the first time we _____ (go) to Italy.

d What _____ (you/do) since we last met?

e _____ (you/ ever/write) a short story?

f I _____ (cut) my finger. It really hurts!

PAST SIMPLE AND PRESENT PERFECT WITH *FOR* AND *SINCE*

5 **Explain the difference between *for* and *since* in the example sentences. Then complete a–d with *for* or *since*, and the present perfect (simple or continuous) or past simple.**

Eve has been studying at this school for six months.

It's six months since we moved into this house.

a I _____ (work) in this school _____ I _____ (begin) my career in teaching.

b We _____ (stand) at this bus stop _____ one o'clock, and there's still no sign of the bus.

c 'How long _____ (you/study) Greek?' 'Only _____ about six months.'

d Tim _____ (be) a professional footballer _____ he _____ (leave) school.

PRESENT PERFECT WITH *STILL, YET, ALREADY* AND *JUST*

6 **Rewrite sentences a–e using the words in brackets and the present perfect tense. You will need to change other words in the sentences.**

a Your mother rang a moment ago. (just)

b The TV programme isn't over yet. (still)

c The students went home about 20 minutes ago. (already)

d The children are still doing their homework. (yet)

e The lesson began a few minutes ago. (just)

7 **Put the verbs in brackets in 1–9 into the present perfect (simple or continuous) or the past simple.**

Antarctica is the coldest, windiest and most remote continent on earth. It [1]_____ (excite) our curiosity for centuries. Those who [2]_____ (be) there talk of the terrible weather, but also of the continent's peace and beauty. Special tourist ships that can break sea ice [3]_____ (make) summer visits for tourists possible in recent years, but scientists [4]_____ (carry out) research on the continent for decades. Permanent bases in Antarctica [5]_____(begin) to be built in the late 1950s, but some daring expeditions [6]_____ (take place) at the start of the 20th century. Since 1958, parties from New Zealand, the USA, Japan and other countries [7]_____ (live) there, exploring and doing research into the geology of the region. Interest in Antarctica remains strong from both tourists and mining companies, but the governments who own territory in Antarctica [8]_____ (so far/be) unwilling to allow too many people to visit the continent. They [9]_____ (always/try) very hard to prevent the environment being damaged by too many visitors.

Antarctica

WORDS WHICH SOUND THE SAME

1 (○ 8) **Listen to eight sentences and underline the word you hear in each pair.**

1 they're   there
2 wear   where
3 sun   son
4 course   coarse
5 we'll   wheel
6 whether   weather
7 here   hear
8 for   four

MULTIPLE CHOICE

2 **Read 1–8 then decide which pair of words a–h you might hear in which extracts.**

a promotion/entrants
b tours/contract
c perfectionist/traditions
d bright/average
e information/download
f artists/recognised
g lifestyle/designed
h booked/charter

1 You hear a man and a woman talking about a story in a newspaper. What was it about?
  A booking a holiday to an unknown destination
  B buying cheap airline tickets
  C ending up at the wrong airport

2 You hear the weather forecast on the radio. What is the weather going to be like tomorrow?
  A It'll be both sunny and overcast during the day.
  B There'll be heavy rain in the afternoon.
  C It'll be cold for the time of year in the evening.

3 You hear a man talking about his laptop. What does he say about having one at home?
  A He wastes too much time on it.
  B He enjoys downloading music.
  C He uses it occasionally for work.

4 You hear part of a radio programme about being famous. What point is the woman making?
  A Anyone can be famous.
  B Even short-term fame isn't possible for everyone.
  C The important thing is to be remembered.

5 You hear a man talking about a cinema competition. What are the rules?
  A You must write two film reviews.
  B Prizes can only be given to children.
  C Prizes must be used at a cinema you select.

6 You hear an advertisement on the radio. What is it for?
  A protective clothing
  B diving and ski equipment
  C alarm clocks

7 You hear part of an interview on the radio. How has the woman's life changed recently?
  A She's been spending more time with her husband.
  B She's been doing less travelling.
  C She's been working on a new film.

8 You hear a woman talking about her job. How does she feel about what she does?
  A She wants to be as efficient as her father.
  B She finds running the business easy.
  C She would rather be a top chef.

3 (○ 9) **You will hear people talking in eight different situations. For questions 1–8 in 2, choose the best answer (A, B or C). Were your predictions in 2 correct?**

> **» EXAM HELPLINE**
>
> **Part 1: Multiple choice**
>
> » Mark your answer on the first listening and check it on the second.
>
> » If you cannot answer a question, leave it and go on to the next one.

> Would you like to be famous? Why?/Why not?
>
> Have you ever won a competition? What did you win?
>
> How important are computers in your life? What do you use them for?

COLLABORATIVE TASK AND DISCUSSION

1 Look at the photos. What do you think the connection is between them? What do you think the examiner might ask you to discuss in the Part 3 task?

2 Read the task on page 106, then close your book and see if you can write the two questions which would appear at the top of the picture sheet in the exam.

3 Match a–g with the photos 1–7.

a water pollution

b noise and air pollution

c traffic congestion

d cutting down trees

e species dying out

f global warming

g getting rid of rubbish

4 **In pairs or groups of three, do the task in 2. Use the words in 3 and some of these phrases.**

Expressing your own opinion

In my opinion, …

Personally, I think …

Actually, I don't think that …

Making a suggestion

Why don't we … ?

What about choosing … ?

I think we should talk about … , don't you?

5 Discuss what kinds of questions the examiner might ask in Part 4. Then look at page 107 and answer the questions. Are they very different from the ones you thought of?

EXPRESSIONS WITH *GET*

Extension p 46 text

1 **What does *get the hang of it* mean in the text on page 46? Unscramble the words in sentences a–e, then match the expressions with the possible meanings 1–5.**

a It can sometimes be difficult to get your message *rossac* on the phone.

b She's late for school every day. I don't know how she manages to get *yawa twih* it.

c Rainy days really get me *nodw*.

d I'll never understand how John managed to get *roghuth* his driving test. He's a terrible driver!

e Why don't we get *tegherot* for a meal sometime?

1 pass

2 make people understand

3 meet

4 make someone feel unhappy

5 do something bad and not be caught.

2 **Choose the correct meaning of the expressions in sentences a–e.**

a Our teacher *gets on well with* all the students in the class.
- is making progress with
- has a friendly relationship with

b Sally never seems to *get around to* doing her homework until it's too late.
- find time for
- think about

c I tried to *get out of* helping Dad to wash the car, but it didn't work.
- suggest
- avoid

d Our dog died last year, and my little sister just can't *get over* it.
- recover from
- get away from

e Paul was *getting nowhere* with his revision.
- had nothing to do
- was not making progress

3 **Answer questions a–e.**

a How well do you get on with your neighbours?

b What would you like to get out of doing, and why?

c What do you do to get over an illness?

d What should you do if you're getting nowhere with your work?

e What kinds of things do you never get around to doing, and why?

DIFFERENT KINDS OF CREATURES

Extension p46 text

4 **Match these words with the creatures 1–6. More than one answer may be possible.**

a mammal

b carnivore

c reptile

d insect

e herbivore

1   2   3

4   5   6

WRITING Extension p46 text

5 **Write a short article comparing the lives of pets and animals in the wild. Mention**

- the advantages and disadvantages of life in the wild.
- the advantages and disadvantages of life as a pet.
- whether life is better for pets or wild animals.

USING ADVERBS Revision p47 ex3

6 **Write the correct form of the words a–h in a suitable place in each sentence.**

a	total	I disagree with what you say.
b	scarce	We had time to finish our lunch.
c	original	This road was built by the Romans.
d	gradual	The procession made its way through the town.
e	free	Deer wander in this area of the national park.
f	special	This book was written for students taking examinations.
g	enthusiastic	The crowds cheered as the film stars began to arrive.
h	furious	They fought to save their house from the fire.

VERBS OF MOVEMENT Revision p47 ex4

7 **Write verbs of movement to match the definitions a–e.**

a	wander	r _ _ _
b	walk at a slow pace	s _ _ _ _ _
c	move or swim in shallow water	p _ _ _ _ _
d	move or push with force	s _ _ _ _
e	move up and down in the water	b _ _

8 Complete sentences a–e with the correct form of the words in 7. Some words are in the noun form.

a Can you see that object _____ up and down in the sea? What is it?

b Tigers still _____ through the jungles of India.

c After the heavy rain, water _____ down the valley and flooded the town.

d Small children love to go for a _____ in the sea.

e Do you fancy a _____ through the park?

MAKING COMPARISONS
Revision page 49 ex6

9 Complete sentences a–e with the correct comparative forms and an adjective of your own.

a Life in a city is not _____ _____ as life on a small island.

b Islands are far _____ _____ than cities.

c The population on some islands isn't _____ _____ as it was two hundred years ago.

d Accommodation is _____ in a small town _____ it is in a large city.

e Most young people think life is _____ _____ in a city than it is on a small island.

EXPRESSIONS WITH *FEEL* Revision p49 ex7

10 Complete the missing words in sentences a–g. The first letter of each word is given.

a I've lived in Greece for years so I really feel p_____ of the community.

b Do you feel l_____ going for a walk?

c The swim in the sea made me feel g_____.

d Do you ever feel i_____ living on a small island?

e David doesn't feel u_____ t_____ going out tonight.

f Please feel f_____ to tell me what you really think.

g Did it feel s_____ to visit your childhood home?

PRESENT PERFECT SIMPLE OR CONTINUOUS? Revision p51 ex 3–4

11 Use these verbs in the present perfect simple or continuous to complete 1–7.

travel	work	present	get
not finish	visit	do	

I [1]_____ wildlife programmes for years now, and I [2]_____ some incredible things. I [3]_____ some amazing places and I [4]_____ very close to some of the most dangerous animals on the planet! We [5]_____ on a new TV series about Africa since April. We [6]_____ all over southern Africa in a really uncomfortable bus and we [7]_____ yet! To be honest, we're all getting tired of being on the road.

PAST SIMPLE OR PRESENT PERFECT?
Revision p51 ex5

12 Complete sentences a–h. Use the past simple or present perfect.

a I _____(live) in my new house for six months.

b When _____ (you/move) to Spain?

c How long _____ (you/have) that old bicycle?

d We _____ (buy) a new television last week.

e This is the first time I _____ (ever/see) this film.

f _____ (you/visit) South America before?

g I _____ (go) to that new nightclub last Saturday.

h What _____ (you/do) to your hair? It looks awful!

PRESENT PERFECT WITH *STILL, YET, ALREADY* AND *JUST* Revision page 51 ex6

13 Choose the correct word to complete sentences a–e.

a The match *still / yet* hasn't finished.

b Have you bought the tickets *just / yet*?

c It's too late! I've *already / still* deleted the file.

d Don't take my plate. I haven't finished *already / yet*.

e I'm really sorry. I think I've *just / already* broken your iPod.

MULTIPLE MATCHING

1 Discuss the questions.

a What does *voluntary work* mean?

b Who might do voluntary work, and why?

2 Quickly read the article and match these descriptions with the volunteer jobs the people describe in A–D.

- working with farm animals
- organising charity events
- helping orphaned animals
- helping disabled people

What reasons do people have for doing volunteer jobs?

If you could do a volunteer job, what kind of job would you choose? Why?

3 Read the article again. For questions 1–15, choose from the volunteer jobs (A–D). The jobs may be chosen more than once.

Which volunteer

1 wasn't interested in doing a volunteer job at first?

2 does work that they used to help their family to do?

3 worked on a volunteer project that is no longer available?

4 was invited to become a volunteer?

5 mentions working in a very relaxed atmosphere?

6 admits that the work can sometimes be difficult?

7 receives financial help for transport?

8 felt they were helping others in several different ways?

9 had no difficulty picking out the job they wanted to do?

10 gained self-confidence by doing the volunteer job?

11 does the voluntary work partly to help their future working life?

12 found themselves with a huge variety of jobs to choose from?

13 does a job that many volunteers end up doing for a long time?

14 worked in a place they had thought about visiting?

15 found a job that requires organisational skills?

>> EXAM HELPLINE

Part 3: Multiple matching

>> Pencilling the question number beside the answer in the text will help you to check your answers.

>> Remember that there are usually similar numbers of questions from each text.

Volunteering can be fun!

A _____

1 Around this time last year, I decided I wanted to do something really different. I came across a website for volunteer work. There were lots of adventurous things to do, and many of the projects looked as if they would suit me, but one leapt out at me straight
5 away: an elephant orphanage project in Sri Lanka, a place I had been planning to visit. The project trained handlers to look after orphaned elephants. I'd always admired these beautiful creatures and dreamt of travelling further afield too, so it seemed the perfect choice. I lived in a village near the orphanage for three
10 weeks with a family who were lovely and welcoming. We got on really well, despite not speaking the same language. When it came to the elephants, I can hardly find words to describe them. Each of the volunteers was given an elephant to look after – in no time at all, I learned to feed, bathe and ride my elephant. It
15 was the chance of a lifetime because the particular project we were working on no longer exists.

B _____

I was first approached by a teacher at college about sports volunteering, which means helping disabled or disadvantaged youth groups play sports. It wasn't a particularly happy
20 time in my life just then, and I also had very little free time because of my other commitments at college. Despite my doubts, I rather reluctantly decided to attend a volunteer session because I felt it might be a useful experience. There I met children from very different backgrounds. They were
25 all eager to learn and get fit, and I discovered that I really enjoyed teaching them. Soon, I found myself going two or three times a week! I felt I was doing something constructive in giving something back to the community and inspiring others. I realised that sport could become a way of teaching
30 disadvantaged children about other aspects of everyday life. The more I volunteered and coached, the more my own self-esteem rose. Sports volunteering picked me up when I was a bit low. I'm a professional sports coach now, and volunteering has vastly improved my own coaching abilities.

C

35 I'm studying events management at university. Last
year I was looking for a role that would help me
further my future career in the music industry, so
volunteering to be part of a charity music festival was
just what I needed. Charity concerts are an amazing
40 idea, and they really help to raise money for many
deprived areas of the world. I was really pleased to be
involved in a small way in three festivals we organised
last year, and after those events, I wanted to take on
a bigger role this year. Although it takes up a lot of
45 my study time, it's a great introduction to the world of
music. Like any job with responsibility, there are times
when things get stressful – but I don't know of any
jobs that don't involve stress. We're already making big
plans for this year's events, and I hope everyone will
50 soon be talking about how much of an effect our work
is having.

D

I've been volunteering at a city farm for a few years
now. I was training to be a vet at college when I first
came here on work experience, and now they can't
55 get rid of me! Some volunteers have been coming
back to the farm for years – they love the place. It's a
really laid-back environment, and the people are really
friendly. City farms provide a service to the community
and to schools. Children come to find out how to
60 look after and feed animals, and they learn how farm
animals should be treated. Anyone can be a volunteer
on a city farm – you don't need any experience. You
don't get paid, but it doesn't cost you anything either
and you even get your travel expenses paid. My
65 parents have a small farm in the countryside so I'm
used to looking after animals. I'd like to run a city farm
myself some day, but that's not why I come here – it's
just for my own pleasure.

PHRASAL VERBS WITH *LOOK*

4 *Look after* and *look for* appear in the text. What do
they mean? Match the phrasal verbs with *look* in
sentences a–e with the meanings 1–5.

  a Could you *look through* this volunteer job application
and make sure I've filled it in correctly?

  b I'm *looking into* the possibility of working in another
country.

  c Can you *look up* the word 'self-esteem' for me?

  d My grandfather's someone everyone *looks up to*.

  e When I *look back on* my childhood, I feel happy.

  1 find information, e.g in a book or on the internet

  2 think about the past

  3 respect

  4 examine carefully

  5 investigate

LIE AND *LAY*

5 *Laid-back* appears in the text. What does it mean?
Complete the table with the missing parts of the
verbs.

Infinitive	Past simple	Present participle	Past participle
to lie (be extended/ situated)	....	....	....
to lie (not tell the truth)	....	....	....
to lay (put)	....	....	....

6 Use the correct form of the verbs in 5 to complete
sentences a–e.

  a Don't believe Brad. He always _____ to people.

  b The empty road _____ in front of me.

  c Paris _____ on the River Seine.

  d Have you _____ the table yet? It's nearly time for
dinner.

  e Instead of _____ there doing nothing, why don't
you do your homework?

ARTICLE BASED ON A SET BOOK

1 **Mario has read a book of short stories called *Ghost Stories*. Read an extract from one of the stories and answer the questions.**

   a Where was Giles?

   b Why was it difficult for him to see clearly?

   c What may have saved Giles's life?

   d Who had shown him the route?

   e What do you think happened next?

The Stranger in the Mist

Giles walked fast. The mist had become thicker than before, but the path was a good one. From time to time he checked his route on the map. Soon the path led him down a very steep hillside. In the mist, Giles could see only a few feet ahead so he moved very carefully. Suddenly his foot turned on a sharp stone and he almost fell. That stone probably saved his life. It flew up from under his feet and rolled down the steep path. He heard it rolling faster and faster, then the noise stopped. A few seconds later Giles heard a crash as the stone hit the ground hundreds of feet below. The path had led him to the edge of a cliff! Giles picked up another stone and dropped it. Again he heard the distant crash as it fell over the cliff. He looked at the map again. There was no cliff on the route that the old man had shown him. For the first time, Giles became seriously worried. He sat down miserably on a large rock, took out his pipe, and found a match to light it. 'Well,' he thought, 'I'll just have to sit and wait for the mist to clear.'

2 From the choice of two questions, Mario has decided to answer exam question (a) below. He needs to write 120–180 words. From the list a–f, choose three main points which you think he will concentrate on in his article.

a the writer's personality

b what happens to the characters in the story

c the historical period the book is set in

d how the reader gets involved in the story

e how the story ends

f why the story is so exciting

Answer one of the following two questions on the title below.

Ghost Stories – Oxford Bookworms Collection

(a) 'This is such an exciting story that you will not be able to put it down.' Write an article for your class magazine, saying whether you agree with this statement or not.

(b) Write a composition for your class magazine, saying whether the characters in the short story you have read seem to be real or imaginary.

Write (a) or (b) above your article.

3 Read Mario's article, ignoring the gaps. Were your predictions in 2 correct? Which two verbs in paragraphs 2 and 3 would be better in the past perfect tense? Why?

(a)

GHOST STORIES
Oxford Bookworms Collection

Read this if you dare!

¹_____ I enjoyed all the short stories, the most exciting was *The Stranger in the Mist*. It is about a man called Giles ²_____ went to Wales on holiday. Giles was interested in geology, and one day he went walking in the mountains but got lost in the mist.

An old man with a dog gave Giles a map ³_____ he could find his way back home. ⁴_____, as you read, you slowly realise that the man gave Giles a very old map ⁵_____ no longer showed the real path.

The story is exciting ⁶_____ you want to know who the man was, and ⁷_____ you cannot put the book down. You imagine that you are lost like Giles. You think that you have met a helpful old man, ⁸_____ , the next minute, you nearly fall over an enormous cliff. You are afraid, ⁹_____ he was, ¹⁰_____ he realised that he nearly died on the mountain. You want to get to the bottom of the mystery so you read on.

LINK WORDS

4 Use these link words to complete 1–10 in Mario's article.

when	which	as
so that	because	then
for that reason	although	who
however		

EXPRESSIONS WITH *BOTTOM*

5 What does the expression *get to the bottom of* in Mario's article mean? Underline the expressions with *bottom* in sentences a–e, then match them with the meanings 1–5.

a We cleaned the house from top to bottom.

b Sam started at the bottom of his profession.

c Our football team came bottom of the league last year.

d The bottom has fallen out of the second-hand car market.

e I'm determined to get to the bottom of these unexplained events.

1 in the last position

2 completely

3 solve or understand a mystery

4 trade has collapsed

5 in the lowest position or job

WRITING ABOUT A SET BOOK

6 Using the ideas and vocabulary in this section, write an article of 120–180 words about an exciting story you have read. Answer exam question (a) or (b) in 2.

> **» EXAM HELPLINE**
>
> **Part 2: Writing about a set text**
>
> » Read both questions, then choose the one that you think you can do best. (In the exam the questions will be about different texts.)
>
> » Make a list of the points to include, then decide which order you will put them in.
>
> » Try to make your article interesting and informative for the target reader.
>
> » Use the *Writing guide* on page 121.

OPEN CLOZE

» EXAM HELPLINE

Part 2: Open cloze

» After reading the text through quickly, read it again carefully sentence by sentence (not line by line) to get an idea of what the missing words might be.

» Be careful of spelling, but don't worry about using capital letters.

» Check your completed text by reading for overall sense.

1 Read the text, ignoring the gaps. Find out why the natural disaster occurred and how the emergency services managed to rescue people.

2 For questions 1–12, read the text again and think of the word which best fits each gap. Use only one word in each gap.

EMERGENCY SERVICES WIN THROUGH

Exhausted and soaking wet, but able to joke ⁰*about* their ordeal, several local families were recovering at a local school last night ¹_____ being rescued from rising flood waters by a coastguard helicopter. ²_____ was the end of a 12-hour operation to lift people ³_____ safety, and residents were full of praise for the emergency services ⁴_____ had rescued them. After four days of torrential rain in southern England, the River Severn finally overflowed ⁵_____ banks, effectively cutting ⁶_____ any means of escape. Some residents scarcely had time to climb onto their rooftops to get away from the water swirling around the ground floors of their homes.

They could do little else ⁷_____ wait for the emergency services to arrive. One by ⁸_____, people were lifted into a helicopter overhead. The rescue attempt was made even ⁹_____ dangerous by strong winds. The area around Tewkesbury is well-known for flooding ¹⁰_____ it is low-lying, but the floods were much worse than forecasters had predicted. The problem now will be ¹¹_____ to house local residents while the damage is being assessed. Some residents may have to live in caravans ¹²_____ they have their houses repaired and redecorated. It may be some time before they are able to return to them.

CAUSATIVE USE OF *HAVE*

3 Complete the dialogues using these verbs and the correct form of the causative use of *have*.

decorate	service	take out	cut
~~dry-clean~~	repair		

Example:

A This jacket is really dirty.

B You should *have it dry-cleaned*.

1 A Is the car you're selling in good working order?

  B Yes, we _____ regularly.

2 A Have you _____?

  B Yes, I was fed up with having long hair.

3 A This tooth is really hurting me.

  B Maybe you'll have to _____.

4 A Our living room looks terrible.

  B Well, why don't we _____?

5 A What's wrong with your watch?

  B It's just stopped working. Do you know anywhere where I could _____?

TEST YOUR KNOWLEDGE: THE PAST PERFECT

Correct any incorrect statements about the past perfect.

a It is rarely used in English.

b It is used for an action which happened before another in the past.

c It does not have a continuous form.

d The negative form is *hadn't* or *had not* + the past participle.

ORDERING EVENTS

4 Beginning with the example, put events a–h from the text in the order that they happened.

a The emergency services arrived. ☐

b A nearby river burst its banks. ☐

c People were winched to safety. ☐

d It rained continuously for four days. 1

e Residents were able to joke about their experience. ☐

f People waited to be rescued. ☐

g Residents were taken to a local school. ☐

h People had to climb onto their rooftops. ☐

PAST SIMPLE OR PAST PERFECT?

5 Combine the sentences in a–d using one verb in the past simple, one in the past perfect, and the words in brackets. Make any other necessary changes.

Example: (just after)

The water reached a depth of two metres.

The windows shattered.

Just after the water had reached a depth of three metres, the windows shattered.

a (after)

The residents were eventually rescued.

The residents were trapped on their rooftops for 12 hours.

b (because)

The rescue workers were relieved.

The rescue workers saw the residents on the rooftops.

c (who)

The families were grateful to the rescue services.

The rescue services took them to safety.

d (because)

The residents moved into caravans.

The flood waters damaged their homes.

PAST PERFECT SIMPLE OR CONTINUOUS?

6 Which verb in italics suggests that the action lasted for some time? Put the verbs in brackets in sentences a–f into the past perfect simple or continuous.

Example: The police *had been questioning* local people in the area where the man *had been attacked*.

a The morning after the lorry _____ (overturn) on the motorway, drivers were full of praise for the emergency services, who _____ (work) all through the night to clear the road.

b A spokesperson at the local hospital, where rescuers _____ (take) some residents for a check-up, said that everyone was well.

c We _____ (walk) for several hours when we suddenly realised that we were lost.

d My car, which I _____ (park) near the river, was swept away.

e Local farmers were described as heroes because they _____ (try) all night to save their livestock.

f Local residents were exhausted after they _____ (work) all weekend to try and save what they could from their flooded houses.

SENTENCE COMPLETION

1 (○10) **Listen to the sentences and find words that mean the same as a–e.**

a reached a point in my life

b succeed in doing something

c continue with what you are doing

d really terrified

e relaxed

2 (○11) **You will hear an interview with Molly Thompson, who went on an unusual horseback ride. For questions 1–10, complete the sentences.**

Would you consider doing what Molly did? Why?/ Why not?

What would you like to do if you could take some time off work or studying?

MOLLY'S NEW ZEALAND HORSEBACK RIDE

Molly did the ride to raise money for a
1_____.

It took Molly 2_____ to complete the trip.

She covered a distance of 3_____.

Her companions on the trip were her cousin, some 4_____ and four horses.

The problems she had at the beginning were rain and not having enough 5_____.

Setting out one day without a 6_____ was one foolish mistake that she made.

Crossing a 7_____ was her most frightening experience.

She celebrated New Year by 8_____.

The experience taught her to 9_____ herself.

Molly would like to do a 10_____ in the future.

PERSONAL INFORMATION

1 Match expressions a–e with the correct prepositions. Use the expressions (as appropriate) to say how you feel about the activities in photos 1–6 below.

Example: *I'm not very keen on reading books.*

a am (not) very keen	about
b am (not particularly) interested	on
c am (not) very fond	with
d am mad	in
e get fed up	of

2 Are these candidates' replies good ones? Why?/Why not?

> What's your favourite sport, Sergio?

> Well, I'm quite keen on team sports, but what I really enjoy is swimming. Actually, I don't mind watching other kinds of sports on TV, but I'd rather take part in them myself.

> Maria, what kind of music do you like?

> I like music a lot. I like modern music and I like some other kinds of music.

3 Work in pairs. Use expressions a–d to talk about your preferences in 1–4.

a I prefer … to … .

b I'd rather (do/have) … than … .

c I like … more than … .

d I don't like … as much as … .

1 see a film/a play

2 listen to classical music/modern music

3 eat Italian food/Chinese food

4 do an outdoor job/an indoor job

4 Use these expressions (as appropriate) to expand upon the comments you made in 3.

Example: *To tell you the truth, I don't really like plays.*

a To tell you the truth, I love/(don't) like …

b To be honest, I find … boring/interesting.

c Actually, I can't stand …

d … bores me stiff.

e What I really enjoy is …

f As a matter of fact, I don't mind …

5 Tell a partner what you like and dislike doing at the weekend and during the holidays.

6 One word is missing in each of sentences a–f. Put in the missing words.

a I'm not particularly interested the cinema.

b As a matter fact, I don't mind listening to the radio.

c What I really enjoy eating fast food.

d I prefer pop music classical music.

e Actually, football bores stiff.

f To tell truth, I can't stand shopping.

PHRASAL VERBS WITH *LOOK*
Extension p57 ex4

1 Use these phrasal verbs with look in the correct form to complete sentences a–h. You may need to add other words.

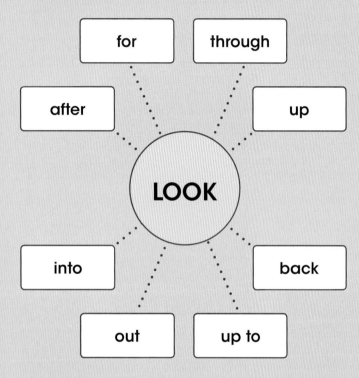

a If you _____ your glasses, they're beside the telephone.

b I'm _____ the possibility of becoming a writer.

c When people _____ on their childhood, they usually remember the good times.

d Who's going _____ your dog while you're away?

e It's important to _____ your written work before handing it in to be marked.

f One person I really _____ is my grandmother – she's amazing for her age.

g _____! That motorbike nearly hit our car.

h I don't understand that word, but I can _____ in the dictionary.

LIE AND LAY Revision p57 ex5

2 Choose the correct form of *lie* or *lay* (a, b or c) to complete sentences 1–5.

1 Giovanni said he didn't come to school because he felt ill, but he might have been _____.
   a lied   b lain   c lying

2 London _____ on the River Thames.
   a lays   b lies   c is lying

3 Maria has _____ the table for four people, but there are five for dinner tonight.
   a lay   b lied   c laid

4 You can't be tired! You _____ around doing nothing all morning.
   a are laying   b have been lying   c have lied

5 Before you paint those walls, can you _____ this sheet on the floor to protect the carpet?
   a lie   b lying   c lay

WRITING Extension p58 text

3 Write a paragraph (about 150 words) describing a time when someone tried to help you to do something. Say
– why you needed help.
– what the person did to help you.
– whether the help was useful or not.

LINK WORDS Revision p59 ex4

4 Use these link words to complete sentences a–h.

because	then	for that reason
although	when	who
as	so that	

a The film was about a woman _____ decided to hitchhike around the world.

b I came to study in England _____ I could really learn the language properly.

c _____ I've never been to Egypt, I've always been interested in the country's culture.

d I put my key in the door, opened it, _____ crept quietly up the stairs.

e I bought a single ticket _____ I'm getting a lift back to town with a friend.

f The passengers were bored, _____ I myself was, with the long journey.

g I've never liked circuses, so _____ I decided not to take the kids to see one.

h _____ we arrived at the cinema, we discovered that the film had already started.

EXPRESSIONS WITH *BOTTOM* Revision p59 ex5

5 Complete the missing words in sentences a–e. The first letter of each word is given.

a Unfortunately, our team c_____ bottom of the league last year.

b I'd like to g_____ to the bottom of this matter once and for all.

c Yesterday I cleaned my room from t_____ to bottom.

d The bottom has f_____ out of the housing market. Maybe it will pick up later in the year.

e Many successful businessmen and women have s_____ at the bottom and worked their way up.

PHRASAL VERBS WITH *CUT* Extension p60 text

6 What do the phrasal verbs in italics mean in sentences a–d? Use the correct form of the phrasal verbs to complete sentences 1–4.

a We will have to *cut back on* our spending if we want to go on holiday this year.

b I phoned Bill last night, but we were *cut off* in the middle of our conversation.

c You'll have to *cut out* sugar from your diet if you want to lose weight.

d Please don't *cut in* when I'm speaking!

1 One member of the debating team kept on _____ while the others were talking.

2 Is there anything we could _____ to try and save a little money?

3 I tried to shorten my composition by _____ one of the paragraphs.

4 The lights aren't working. I think the electricity must have been _____.

CAUSATIVE USE OF *HAVE* Revision p61 ex3

7 Complete dialogues 1–5 using these verbs and the causative use of *have*. You may need to add pronouns.

test	shorten	plant
paint	cut	

1 A: The garden looks great!
   B: Yes, I've _____ some new trees _____.

2 A: Do you like my hair?
   B: Yes, I do. Have you _____?

3 A: This skirt is far too long.
   B: Why don't you _____?

4 A: _____ your room _____?
   B: Yes, I have. Do you like the colour?

5 A: Can you read that car number plate over there?
   B: No, I can't. Do you think I should go and _____ my eyes _____?

PAST SIMPLE OR PAST PERFECT?
Revision p61 ex5

8 Use one verb in the past simple and the other in the past perfect to complete sentences a–g.

a I _____ (know) that I _____ (make) several mistakes in my maths test.

b I _____ (buy) the shoes that I _____ (see) in the shop the day before.

c Although I _____ (never/ride) an elephant before, I _____ (seem) to know exactly how to do it.

d For one awful moment, we _____ (think) we _____ (forgot) our passports.

e We _____ (spend) so many great holidays in Spain that we eventually _____ (decide) to buy a flat there.

f Yesterday Martin _____ (tell) me that he and Susan _____ (got) engaged.

g After I _____ (finish) school, I _____ (go) on a trip to the USA.

9 Put the verbs in brackets into the correct active or passive form of the past simple or the past perfect simple.

Last night the emergency services [1]_____ (call) to a fire which [2]_____ (start) in a hotel in the town centre 20 minutes earlier. When they [3]_____ (arrive), they [4]_____ (find) that most of the guests [5]_____ (already/evacuate) from the hotel. Unfortunately, one elderly guest, who [6]_____ (not/hear) hotel staff banging on his door just after the outbreak of the fire, [7]_____ (be) still in the building. Luckily, firefighters [8]_____ (manage) to rescue him just in time. Apparently, the man [9]_____ (be) a firefighter himself before retiring ten years ago, so he [10]_____ (know) that he was in safe hands.

MULTIPLE CHOICE

1 Read the article and find out how the writer organised her holiday to Ecuador.

> How much do you think you can really learn about a country by visiting it on a package tour? Do you think that travel networking is a good way to visit a country? Why?/Why not?

2 Read the article again. For questions 1–8, choose the answer (A, B, C or D) which you think fits best according to the text.

1 What is the taxi driver suggesting in paragraph 1?
   - A He is willing to take the backpackers anywhere they want to go.
   - B He is happy to suggest sights the backpackers might want to see.
   - C He is aware of the route that backpackers normally follow.
   - D He is bored with driving backpackers along the same busy route.

2 What is the writer saying about backpackers in paragraph 2?
   - A They spend more time travelling than sightseeing.
   - B They are more interested in other countries than their own.
   - C They are not very organised when it comes to travelling.
   - D They tend to follow in the footsteps of their fellow-travellers.

3 What comment does the writer make about travel-networking websites?
   - A They are not thought to be very reliable.
   - B They are popular with some travellers.
   - C They are used mostly by backpackers.
   - D They aren't as good as people say they are.

4 What does the writer say about the website she contacted in paragraph 4?
   - A It helps travellers in a variety of ways.
   - B It provides its services free of change.
   - C It offers reductions on some forms of travel.
   - D It has been established for quite some time.

5 What does the writer say she regrets in paragraph 5?
   - A being restricted to travelling by bus
   - B spending so much time in one place
   - C being unable to change arrangements
   - D having to plan so much at the last minute

6 The writer uses the phrase 'bowled over by Loja' in line 55 to show that she was
   - A amazed by the city.
   - B curious about the city.
   - C puzzled by the city.
   - D disappointed by the city.

7 What comment does the writer make about Loja?
   - A It attracts crowds of tourists.
   - B Its recent history is interesting.
   - C There are a lot of attractive places in the city.
   - D It's a great place if you like dancing.

8 Overall, how does the writer feel about travel networking?
   - A astounded by its success
   - B frustrated by its limitations
   - C reluctant to repeat the experience
   - D generally satisfied with the results it produced

›› EXAM HELPLINE

Part 1: Multiple choice

›› Always check that <u>all</u> the information in the answer is correct.

›› When answering a question about a word or phrase (Question 6), make sure you read the text before and after to help you understand the meaning.

PHRASAL VERBS WITH *HANG*

3 The phrasal verb *hang out* appears in the article. What does it mean? Match the phrasal verbs in sentences a–e with meanings 1–5.

a Those children are always *hanging about* at the corner of the street.

b If you *hang on* a minute, I'll see if John's in.

c Jane wanted to say something, but for some reason she *hung back*.

d Please don't *hang up* – we need to talk about this now.

e *Hang on* tight – the roller coaster is about to start.

1 end a phone conversation

2 wait

3 hold onto something

4 stand around not doing much

5 hesitate because you're nervous

Going local in Ecuador

'Let me guess. You're going to the middle of the world,' says the Quito taxi driver, turning to the English backpackers in the back seat, while simultaneously negotiating the mid-morning traffic. He's right first time.

The equator is one of the Ecuadorian capital's biggest attractions – even though GPS devices have recently revealed the much-photographed line to be off-centre by over 200 metres. 'Then, after Quito, you're going to Baños and then ...' He reels off the standard tour of Ecuador, a spot-on prediction that makes the girls in the back laugh out loud.

Backpacking has changed. What was supposed to open your eyes to new countries and new cultures, these days often involves hanging out with other travellers, often from your own country, while following the same carbon-copy route, Lonely Planet tourist guide checklist in hand. There's no point in being snobby about it – many of us have done the same. But this time when it came to planning a fast-moving, three-month trip around Central and South America, I decided to take a different approach. I wanted to find out whether travel-networking websites live up to their reputation. Serving as worldwide directories of people willing to share their time with passing travellers, they have already become quite popular. Yet surprisingly few backpackers have heard of them – even fewer have put them to the test.

My first experience of travel networking came last year when I organised a weekend in Berlin packed with social engagements with people I had met online. But then I decided to take up the biggest challenge to date. Over the next three months, I would be building my entire trip around meetings I'd prearranged online with local people, who I hoped would help me to explore their countries beyond the guidebooks.

How then, did I end up in a taxi with people I met at my hostel taking the stereotypical trip to the 'Middle of the Earth'? I was actually en route to my first local contact, who was working for a website that was founded quite recently. The site offers one approved contact per country. There's a charge for using it, of course, but the idea is that the contacts are rather like tourist guides: they are there to assist you with travel plans, share contacts, take you on tours and help you negotiate discounts at hotels. The meeting was everything I'd expected, and I was sorry when at the end of our tour we had to say goodbye.

My next contact gave me an insight into a specific side of the city: its music. I checked out a list of musical venues but was unable to spend any time in one I particularly wanted to go to because I'd already booked my bus to my next destination. I discovered early on that one drawback of such a tight schedule is that there's little room for manoeuvre.

My bus was heading to Loja, a small southern city that caught my eye. It was proclaimed the country's 'cultural and musical capital', with a famed music conservatory and a reputation for churning out artists. I was bowled over by Loja – dating back to 1548, it's one of the country's oldest and most interesting cities. With my contact, I saw grand city gates give way to colourful historical wall paintings and picturesque colonial plazas bordered by shady sidewalks. Hidden doors led to mini art galleries, and teenagers rehearsed folk dances in the streets. It was a shame to leave Loja, but I had to continue my journey and meet my next contacts.

After visiting Guayaquil, I made my way to Panama City, where I finished my journey – and where I met my last contact. She was fresh from her experience of working as an extra on the latest James Bond movie, which was currently on location. By now, we'd exchanged so many emails, she felt like an old friend.

So how do I regard website networking now? Definitely not negatively – it's certainly a different way of seeing the world.

REVIEW

1 Decide if these statements about a review are true or false.

a It is often written for a magazine, newspaper or website.

b It should give a clear impression of what the item being discussed is really like.

c Its main purpose is to describe and express other people's opinions about something, and not your own ideas.

d It should include a recommendation to the reader.

2 Read the exam question and underline what you think are the most important words or phrases.

You have seen this advertisement on an English language website called Holiday Experiences.

Wanted — holiday reviews!

Have you just been on holiday?
Feel like telling us about it?

If so, write us a review of 120–180 words.
Mention the location, the type of holiday and the accommodation, and say whether you would recommend the holiday to others.

We are offering prizes for the best reviews.

Write your review.

3 Read the review opposite that Andreas sent in to the website. Has Andreas

a mentioned all the points in the question?

b organised his writing well?

c used a good range of structures and vocabulary?

d produced writing without too many mistakes? (Can you find the mistakes that he has made?)

e used the right kind of style for the task?

f fully informed his target readers?

Last October we went on Nile cruise. It was one of the most interesting holidays I have ever had. Our holiday began in Luxor. We visited the huge temple of Karnak and the Valley of the Kings, which has got a lot of impressing tombs.

After that, we flew to Aswan. There we board a ship and cruised down the River Nile back to Luxor. The cabins and the food on board were excellent. It was very peaceful on the river and the weather was fantastic. It was not too hot or too cold.

Every day, we stopped at a different place and visited the amazing temples and other interesting sites along the riverbank. We had a very good guide, and that made all the difference. I had studied some Egyptian history at school, but seeing the country was much fascinating than reading about it.

So if you are keen on travelling and want to visit somewhere with a lot of history, I would recommend going to Egypt. It is a holiday you will certainly never forget.

PREPOSITION + -ING

4 Complete sentences a–e using these prepositions and the -ing form of the verbs in brackets.

of	about	in	with	for

a Most people are interested _____ (learn) about other cultures.

b I'm not very fond _____ (lie) on a beach doing nothing.

c You cannot blame people _____ (want) to relax after a day's sightseeing.

d I'm fed up _____ (go) to the same place on holiday every year.

e I am worried _____ (miss) my flight connection.

-ING OR INFINITIVE?

5 Want to visit and recommend going appear in the review. Complete the table with these verbs.

want	can't help	finish	decide
keep on	manage	hope	enjoy
imagine	practise	intend	suggest

verb + -ing	verb + infinitive
_____	_____
_____	_____
_____	_____
_____	_____
_____	_____
_____	_____
_____	_____

6 Complete sentences a–f so that they are true for you, using either -ing or an infinitive.

a I can't help _____.

b I've finished _____.

c I've decided _____.

d I haven't managed _____.

e I try to practise _____.

f Next year I intend _____.

EXPRESSIONS WITH *MAKE*

7 *Made all the difference* appears in the review. What does it mean? Match the expressions with *make* in sentences a–e with definitions 1–5.

a It's easy to *make a habit of* getting up late.

b I can't quite *make out* what that building is over there.

c I can't *make up my mind* where to go on holiday.

d We need to *make the most of* our leisure time.

e Many people have to *make do with* one short holiday a year.

1 decide

2 get used to

3 gain as much advantage as possible

4 manage to see

5 manage with something which is not satisfactory

WRITING A REVIEW

8 You have been asked to write a 120–180 word review of a holiday you have been on. Mention where you went, the type of holiday you went on and the accommodation. Say whether you would recommend the holiday to others.

> ## » EXAM HELPLINE
>
> **Part 2: Review**
>
> » Remember that the aim of a review is to give the reader a clear impression of what you are writing about.
>
> » Include your opinions as well as writing descriptions.
>
> » Always end your review with a recommendation.
>
> » Use the *Writing guide* on page 122.

WORD FORMATION

1 Have you ever had a holiday trip that turned out to be a disappointment? What happened?

2 Read the text about a husky safari, ignoring the gaps and the words in capitals, and find out what the family and their guide had to do at night.

Overnight husky safari

Sliding across a ⁰ _____frozen_____ lake in the Norwegian wilderness, the stars are ¹_____ above you as a team of huskies pulls you through the ²_____ landscape. You might think that this sounds like ³_____. Well, it wasn't!

◄ FREEZE

◄ TWINKLE

◄ FANTASY
◄ PERFECT

It was a winter holiday treat for the whole family, and we were all looking forward to spending the night in a log cabin. At first, it was lots of fun – the huskies dashed along ⁴_____, throwing us about on the sleds. 'How could anyone possibly ⁵_____ this,' we thought. And then, suddenly, ⁶_____ fell – and it was only three o'clock! Four hours later, we were still sledding – cold, and by then, suffering from ⁷_____ and hunger.

◄ EXCITE

◄ LIKE
◄ DARK

◄ EXHAUST

'Don't worry!' shouted the guide. He told us that we would soon be at our ⁸_____. But it felt as if we were going round and round in circles. Then, through the gloom, a cabin came slowly into view. 'It must be ours,' we thought – but the guide said that it wasn't and started to look worried. One hour later, to our horror, the guide informed us that we were lost. We decided we had no ⁹_____ but to turn back and break into the cabin that we had passed, and spend the night there. Although the freezing cabin was extremely ¹⁰_____, it was certainly better than being outside!

◄ DESTINED

◄ ALTERNATE

◄ COMFORT

3 Read the text again. Use the word given in capitals at the end of some of the lines to form a word that fits in the gap in the same line.

TEST YOUR KNOWLEDGE: REPORTED SPEECH

Correct sentences a–e.

a My brother asked me I wanted to go on holiday with him.

b A woman asked me what time did the train leave.

c Our neighbour suggested us to go to Portugal on holiday.

d Ted told that he couldn't come to the party.

e Susan asked me whether I want to go to the beach.

REPORTING STATEMENTS

4 When reporting statements, you usually need to change the tense of the verb in the statement you are reporting. Turn sentences a–e into reported statements, making any other necessary changes.

a 'The tickets will arrive tomorrow,' said the travel agent.

b 'Tourists have come here from all over the world,' said the guide.

c 'We're going to visit the Pyramids this morning,' said a young man.

d 'Our hotel won a top award last year,' said the owner.

e 'The coaches are leaving at 6 p.m. today,' said the guide.

5 If what is reported is still true, or the speaker uses a reporting verb in the present, we don't have to change the tense of the verb. Report statements a–d, making changes to pronouns and possessive adjectives.

a 'My sister is working on a cruise ship.'

Paul says _____.

b 'We always go skiing in April.'

My cousins said _____.

c 'I've had a good season this year.'

The restaurant owner says _____.

d 'My father was an Olympic skier.'

Lucy says _____.

REPORTING IMPERATIVES

6 Report sentences a–e using *asked* or *told*.

a 'Please don't forget to pack your swimming things.'

Ben's mother _____.

b 'Don't make so much noise!'

The children's father _____.

c 'Please come shopping with me tomorrow.'

My friend Rob _____.

d 'Can you help me to book a hotel on the internet?'

My sister _____.

e 'Be quiet, students!'

The teacher _____.

REPORTING QUESTIONS

7 You have to change the word order when reporting direct questions. Complete reported questions a–e. What word do you add in c and d?

a 'Where is the information desk?'

I asked the man where _____.

b 'How long have you been working for this car hire company?'

He asked the woman how long _____.

c 'Are you interested in art?'

Bob asked Maria _____.

d 'Are you going to buy some new clothes for your holiday?'

Ian asked me _____.

e 'What time does the flight land?'

The passenger asked the steward _____.

REPORTING VERBS

8 Match the reporting verbs a–f with structures 1–4. Then use them in sentences of your own.

Example: *Pete threatened to tell the teacher I hadn't done my homework.*

a threatened	1 the infinitive form
b suggested	2 *whether, if* or a question word
c wondered	3 *that* + another sentence
d complained	4 the *-ing* form of the verb
e offered	
f wanted to know	

MULTIPLE MATCHING

1 Discuss the questions.

a Do you think that we will need to build more motorways in the future? Why?/Why not?

b Should drivers have to pay for using motorways?

» EXAM HELPLINE

Part 3: Multiple matching

» You may wish to make a note of your answers the first time you listen and complete the answer sheet the second time.

» Remember that changing one of your answers may affect another answer.

2 (○12) You will hear five different people talking about a plan to build a motorway near to where they live. Choose from the list (A–F) what each speaker says. Use the letters only once. There is one extra letter which you do not need to use.

A We shouldn't encourage more traffic and pollution.

B We should charge people to use new roads.

C We have to accept some problems if we want to keep driving.

D Motorways shouldn't be built near to residential areas.

E Traffic noise really affects people's lives.

F We should appreciate being car owners.

Speaker 1	
Speaker 2	
Speaker 3	
Speaker 4	
Speaker 5	

3 (○13) Listen and complete the sentences from each extract with words used to express opinions.

1 *The _____ is that we're living in a modern day and age and we should be pleased we can all have cars – not moaning about where people are driving them!*

2 *To a _____, it doesn't matter whether it's an ordinary road or a motorway which is close to a town or city …*

3 *It's all _____ saying that the increase in the number of cars on the roads means that we'll have total gridlock unless we build more motorways …*

4 *There's _____ in my mind that we have to build more roads to cope with the sheer volume of traffic nowadays.*

5 *I'm not _____ motorways as such, but I do think more could be done to reduce the amount of traffic noise.*

4 Match the expressions in italics in 3 with these meanings.

a I'm not opposed to

b it may seem OK to say

c it's partly true that

d I'm sure

e the really important thing

> How would you feel if a new motorway was going to be built near to where you live?
>
> Do you agree that new motorways are a necessary price to pay for progress?

THE LONG TURN

1 If you were given these two photos in the exam, what do you think the examiner would ask you to talk about? (Remember that written questions will appear at the top of the photos in the exam.)

2 Compare the exam task on page 106 with your ideas in 1.

3 Make a list of the advantages and disadvantages of using the ways of travelling in the photos. These ideas might help you.

comfort	cost
length of journey	difficulty of journey
organisation needed	facilities while travelling
luggage	scenery

Photo 1	Photo 2
advantages _____ _____	advantages _____ _____
disadvantages _____ _____	disadvantages _____ _____

4 Write a similar table of advantages and disadvantages for these photos.

5 In pairs, take turns to do the exam task in 2, using the pairs of photos in 1 and 4. Stop each other after one minute.

» EXAM HELPLINE

Part 2: The long turn

» Listen carefully to how the examiner introduces the task. This is not part of the questions that appear above the photos.

» Compare the photos – don't simply describe them.

» Use your imagination to make full use of the minute in your long turn.

6 Compare your ideas with another pair of students. Which did you decide was the best way to travel? Why?

7 What question do you think the examiner might ask the listening candidate? Turn to page 107 and find out.

PHRASAL VERBS WITH *HANG*

Revision p66 ex3

1 Complete sentences a–e with the correct form of a phrasal verb with *hang*.

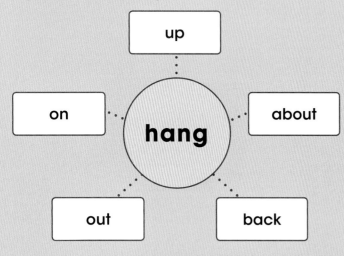

a Don't _____ if you have something you really want to tell me.

b I hate it when people just _____ when they've got the wrong number.

c I like to _____ in the shopping centre with my friends.

d You need to _____ tight or you might fall off the ski lift.

e Those people _____ at the end of the road look a bit suspicious.

WORDS CONNECTED WITH TRAVELLING

Extension p67 text

2 Use the correct form of these words to complete sentences a–h. Use each word only once.

trip	tour	voyage	journey
drive	flight	travel	ride

a The long ocean _____ from Britain to Australia used to take months.

b My mother goes on a lot of business _____ abroad.

c We haven't decided whether we are going to _____ by train or car.

d If you like horses, we could go for a _____ tomorrow.

e Airlines are now offering cut-price _____ to many destinations.

f Let's go by car. It's only a ten-minute _____ from here to the city centre.

g It's worth going on a guided _____ of the city if you want to see the sights.

h How long does your _____ to work take?

EXPRESSIONS WITH *EYE* Extension p67 text

3 What does *open your eyes* mean in the text on page 67? Match these expressions with *eye* with the meanings a–e. Then complete sentences 1–5.

see eye to eye	up to your eyes in
keep an eye on	catch (your) eye
have eyes in the back of your head	

a have a lot to do

b take care of someone or something

c know what's happening all around you

d have the same opinion

e notice

1 James and I get on very well, although we don't always _____.

2 Can you help me out, please? I'm _____ in this paperwork.

3 Could you _____ on the children while I pop out to the shops?

4 I didn't see what happened. I _____, you know!

5 Did anything _____ while you were shopping today?

PREPOSITIONS + *-ING* Revision p69 ex4

4 Complete sentences a–g with the correct form of a suitable verb.

a The students are worried about _____ the test tomorrow.

b I'm not very fond of _____ my holidays in the mountains.

c Please don't blame me for _____ Olivia your secret.

d Do you ever get tired of _____ to the same music all the time?

e I'm fed up with _____ out. Let's go to the theatre tonight instead of staying in.

f Everyone in our family has always been interested in _____ to other countries.

g You haven't got any excuse for _____ me to do all the housework.

-ING OR INFINITIVE? Revision p69 ex5

5 Complete sentences a–e with a suitable verb in the -ing or infinitive form.

a What do you want _____ this weekend?

b If you want to be a pianist, you'll have to practise _____ the piano every evening.

c Did you manage _____ a nice present for Sally?

d Have you all finished _____ your essay?

e The twins are learning _____ French.

EXPRESSIONS WITH *MAKE* Revision p69 ex7

6 Write the missing words to complete sentences a–e.

a Have you made up your _____ what you want to do when you leave school?

b There isn't much food in the fridge. We'll just have to make _____ with what there is.

c You shouldn't make a _____ of staying out late.

d I couldn't make _____ what the notice at the side of the road said.

e We ought to make the _____ of the weather today. It's going to rain tomorrow!

WRITING Extension p70 text

7 Write a 120–180 word review of a terrible day out you had. Mention

– the place you went to.

– what you did there.

– what happened to make it such a terrible day out.

REPORTED SPEECH Revision p71 ex4–7

8 Change sentences a–g into direct speech.

a The manager told the sales assistant to try to be more helpful to customers.

b Anna said she had never won a prize before.

c Peter asked if anyone had seen his sports bag.

d The guests commented that the hotel facilities were excellent.

e Some tourists asked me if I would take a photo of them.

f The guide said that the next tour would take place in half an hour.

g The children complained that they couldn't see anything on the menu they wanted to eat.

REPORTING VERBS Revision p71 ex8

9 Use these verbs to report sentences a–h. You may use some verbs more than once. More than one answer may be possible.

suggested	threatened	wondered
complained	offered	wanted to know

Example:
'Shall we sit near the front?'
One of the tourists *suggested that they sat near the front.*

a 'What time does the show start?'
A member of the audience _____.

b 'I can't see anything from where I'm sitting.'
One tourist _____.

c 'I'll get you a concert programme if you haven't got one.'
The man sitting next to me _____.

d 'Can anybody afford to eat in this restaurant?'
A passer-by _____.

e 'Anyone selling match tickets illegally will be fined.'
A club official _____.

f 'Are you eating in the hotel tonight, Tom?'
A friend _____.

g 'This guide book is dreadful.'
A sightseer _____.

h 'We could visit the modern art museum.'
Ellen _____.

Alpine Adventure

MISSING SENTENCES

1 Match these adjectives with the words a–e to describe the weather conditions in the pictures. Then quickly read the article to check your answers.

| heavy | fine | strong | thick | fluffy |

a drizzle b clouds c fog d wind e rain

1 2 3

4 5

2 Seven sentences have been removed from the article. Choose from the sentences A–H the one which fits each gap (1–7). There is one extra sentence which you do not need to use.

A The fog was so thick that I almost missed a dim light glowing from a chalet which, on closer inspection, turned out to be a cafeteria.

B But, well-practised in mountain walking, I set off at a steady plod past silhouettes of cuckoo clock houses and farms perched above the U-shaped bends in the road.

C I could not go knocking on all the doors so I would simply have to wait.

D The windows rattled and the smoky fog persisted, but it was only 8.30 and I lingered, hoping the sun might dissolve the gloom and present me with a vision of Switzerland.

E But the day ahead was going to be long and strenuous and so I flung off the duvet, packed and crept downstairs.

F But towards the top, my hopes were dashed by fog so thick that a false night seemed to have fallen around me.

G It worked, and like an escaping prisoner I reached the wet pre-dawn street without setting off an alarm.

H It spotted me, but instead of disappearing into the undergrowth, it leapt effortlessly onto a beech log and crouched there as though posing for a wildlife photograph.

1 My watch alarm woke me at five. I lay still, listening for rain. There it was again, out in the darkness, challenging me to stay in bed. **1 E** The front door was locked, and I fumbled behind the desk for a key.
5 I found a jangling jailer's bunch but none of the keys fitted. Using my torch I tiptoed through the kitchen, but the rear exit was also locked. A clock chimed the half hour.

I sat down, wondering whether it would be wise to
10 wake the manageress at 5.30 a.m., but where was she? In the restaurant the trout tank bubbled while above my head the clock ticked away the precious seconds. I shone my torch round the reception area. Something glinted: a solitary brass key on a hook. **2**

15 The steep road did not allow me to begin the day gently. **3** The heavy rain turned to fine drizzle and dim light filtered into the valley. The fluffy clouds turned purple, mauve, then pink, and I could see the river valley stretching away to the east and west, the
20 cattle in its meadows as still as haystacks as they waited for their later dawn. The drizzle ceased and I stopped at a cold clear stream to drink, and sat watching a faint rainbow forming in the west. I was about to set off again when a sudden
25 movement prompted me to stop. At first I thought it might be a squirrel, but the creature which bounded across the road was far too big. It was as large as a domestic cat. I froze. **4** It stared at me with inquisitive black eyes, then, more bored than afraid,
30 glided noiselessly into the wild wood.

The road continued to rise at a steady angle. No vehicles passed me, and the only sounds were of water, the strong wind blowing, and birdsong. My legs no longer ached and my leather boots, stretched by
35 the rain, now fitted my feet. At last I was beginning to enjoy myself, and singing, I gradually gained altitude. I was eager to see the pass from which I would be able to see the Jura mountains. **5**

A rock face became a building; a monstrous ski lodge,
40 its locked doors and shuttered windows showing no lights. The chill was so intense that I continued up the road with my teeth chattering. Where was the top? **6** Its interior had been designed for coach parties and I was the only customer.

45 The owner was using the slack period between seasons to varnish a pine wall while his wife fed their blonde toddler. They were astonished to see me, but agreed to give me coffee. 'Is this the summit?' I asked, and it was. **7** But after four coffees I set off
50 again. At least it was all downhill now, and I walked quickly, anxious to rejoin the visible world again.

> Why do you think people enjoy mountain walking so much?
> What other things can people do in the mountains to keep fit?

VERBS OF MOVEMENT

3 Decide whether the verbs a–i from the article are used to talk about the writer or the creature on the mountain, then match them with meanings 1–9. What are the past forms of a–i?

a fling   f freeze
b creep   g leap
c fumble   h crouch
d tiptoe   i stare
e bound

1 look for a long time with eyes wide open
2 suddenly stop moving (often because of fear)
3 hold or handle something awkwardly
4 rest near the ground with bent knees
5 throw something forcefully
6 walk slowly with heels raised off the ground
7 jump high or a long way
8 move slowly, quietly and carefully
9 move fast, with jumping movements

PHRASAL VERBS WITH *SET*

4 *Set off* appears in the article. What does it mean? Replace the words in italics in a–e with phrasal verbs with *set*. Which verb has the same meaning as *set off*?

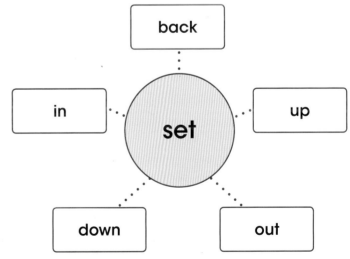

a We *left* on the first stage of our journey in January.
b The bad weather *delayed the progress of* the walking tour by three days.
c Don't plan everything in your head. *Write* your ideas on a piece of paper.
d The company was *established* about ten years ago.
e They were near the summit when the bad weather *started*.

STORY

1 Read the exam question and one of the entries in the competition opposite. Then put the verbs in 1–12 into the correct past tense. Remember to use the past perfect for events which happened before other events in the past.

You have decided to enter a short story competition in a local newspaper. The story must begin with the following words:

The middle-aged man in the seat opposite Jim looked suspicious.

Write a short story of 120–180 words.

2 Number events a–i in the order that they happen in the story.

a A strange man began to stare in Jim's direction. ☐

b The train stopped. ☐

c The man showed the woman his police identification. ☐

d Jim saw a headline in the newspaper. ☐

e The man arrested the dark-haired woman. ☐

f A famous painting was stolen. [1]

g The dark-haired woman smiled at Jim. ☐

h The man asked Jim if he could borrow his newspaper. ☐

i Jim caught the train. ☐

INTERESTING THE READER

3 A successful short story holds the attention of the reader. What does the writer of this story want you to think? What is unexpected about the ending of the story?

USING ADVERBS

4 Adverbs can make your writing more interesting. Underline the adverbs in the story.

THE LANGUAGE OF DESCRIPTION

5 What are adjectives a–j used to describe in the story?

a black

b attractive

c suspicious

d old-fashioned

e grey

f tall

g large

h uncomfortable

i thin

j dark-haired

The middle-aged man in the seat opposite Jim looked suspicious. He was extremely tall and thin, and had a black moustache. He ¹_____ (wear) an old-fashioned tracksuit and carrying a large sports bag. He ²_____ (stare) in Jim's direction ever since the train ³_____ (leave) the station. Jim, who ⁴_____ (write) a college essay on his laptop, ⁵_____ (begin) to feel slightly uncomfortable.

The man ⁶_____ (lean) across and asked Jim if he could borrow his newspaper. Jim ⁷_____ (give) it to him reluctantly. He ⁸_____ (not finish) reading it himself.

He ⁹_____ (only/see) the headline about the theft of a famous painting before boarding the train.

The attractive, dark-haired woman sitting next to Jim with her large, grey briefcase was a completely different matter. She had smiled at Jim when she got on the train and seemed friendly.

The train ¹⁰_____ (stop) abruptly. The woman hurriedly ¹¹_____ (get) up, but the man ¹²_____ (already/stand up) and was now blocking the doorway. 'Not so fast,' the man said, showing her his police identification. 'I'm arresting you for the theft of a Picasso painting from the National Gallery.'

6 **Put the words in descriptions a–d into the correct order.**

a leather jacket a short brown

b a(n) ring diamond expensive-looking

c vase blue Indian a(n) tall

d beautiful with hair a long young blonde woman

PHRASES WITH *LOOK*

7 **The man in the story *looked suspicious*. Match the phrases with *look* in sentences a–g with meanings 1–7.**

a The hotel was *not much to look at*, but the staff were friendly.

b Since winning the talent competition, Susan has *never looked back*.

c Don't *look around*, but I think there's someone famous behind you.

d It's difficult for us to *look ahead* at the moment.

e Don't you think John's beginning to *look his age*?

f You should *look after* yourself instead of thinking about other people all the time.

g I *don't like the look of* that cut. You should see a doctor.

1 continue to be successful

2 take care of

3 think about what might happen in the future

4 be worried by the appearance of something

5 appear as old as you really are

6 turn your head in order to see something

7 be unattractive in appearance

THE POSITION OF ADVERBS

8 **Insert these adverbs in a suitable place in sentences a–g in 7. More than one answer may be possible.**

extremely	straight away	actually
always	incredibly	really

WRITING A SHORT STORY

9 **You have decided to enter a short story competition in a magazine. The story must be 120–180 words and begin with the words below. Include some adverbs and adjectives.**

The lady at the end of the cinema ticket queue looked worried.

›› EXAM HELPLINE

Part 2: Story

›› Before you start writing your story, list the events in the order in which they take place. This doesn't have to be the order you introduce them in the story.

›› Don't make your story too complicated or go off the subject.

›› Ask yourself 'Would I find this story interesting?'

›› Use the *Writing guide* on page 123.

08 USE OF ENGLISH

OPEN CLOZE

1 **When and where do you listen to music? Would you enjoy listening to music while you exercise?**

2 **Read the article below quickly, ignoring the gaps, and find out why listening to music while you exercise could be a good idea.**

3 **For 1–8, think of the word which best fits each gap. Use only one word in each gap.**

Sounds like a winner

If you were running in a marathon, [1]_____ you take your MP3 player with you? Well, it might be a good idea. Runners have used music to help them push through the pain barrier for years, and we now know [2]_____ to make the best use of the advantage it can give you. One expert in sports psychology who has [3]_____ studying the use of music in sport believes [4]_____ of the key benefits is reducing a runner's perception of effort. [5]_____ other words, it makes the task seem easier [6]_____ time appears to go more quickly. And [7]_____ you pick the right tunes, you can synchronise your pace to the music, improving energy efficiency and performance [8]_____ roughly 16 per cent!

TEST YOUR KNOWLEDGE: CONDITIONALS

Match questions a–e with answers 1–5.

a How many different types of conditional are there?

b Which conditional is used to talk about things which might happen in the future?

c Which conditional is used to speculate about what happened in the past?

d In which part of some conditional sentences do we not generally use *will* or *would*?

e What two meanings does the *'d* have in this conditional sentence? *If you'd told me your secret, I'd have kept it to myself.*

1 after *if*

2 four

3 the third

4 *had* and *would*

5 the first

WHICH CONDITIONAL?

4 **Match the conditional sentences a–d with the explanations 1–4.**

a If you boil water, it turns to steam.

b Unless it rains this afternoon, we'll go for a walk.

c If Ted were a millionaire, he'd give all his money away to the poor.

d If Daisy had worked harder, she would have got top marks in the test.

1 This is very unlikely to happen.

2 This is always true.

3 This definitely didn't happen.

4 This may happen.

ZERO OR FIRST CONDITIONAL?

5 **Use the correct form of the verbs in brackets to complete sentences a–f. More than one answer may be possible.**

a If you _____ (drink) too quickly, you may _____ (get) hiccups.

b You _____ (get) soaked if you _____ (go) out in this rain!

c Food _____ (go) bad unless you _____ (keep) it cool.

d If I _____ (finish) doing my homework early, I _____ (go) to the cinema.

e We _____ (stop) and ask someone the way if we _____ (not find) the street.

f If the temperature _____ (fall) below zero, water _____ (freeze).

THE SECOND CONDITIONAL

6 **Which of the second conditional examples in sentences 1–3 is used to**

a give someone advice?

b talk about something which can never happen?

c talk about something which is unlikely to happen?

1 If I were President, I would live a life of luxury.

2 If I were you, I would give up the idea of being an entertainer.

3 If I were an animal, I'd like to be a dolphin.

THE THIRD CONDITIONAL

7 **Answer the questions a–b about sentences 1–2.**

1 If Patsy hadn't got up late, she wouldn't have missed the plane.

   a Did Patsy get up late?

   b Did she miss the plane?

2 If Patsy had heard her alarm clock, she would have arrived in time to catch the plane.

   a Did Patsy hear her alarm clock?

   b Did she arrive in time to catch the plane?

8 **Complete and match the sentence halves in a–e and 1–5 to make third conditional sentences.**

a Paul _____ (not take part) in the Olympic Games

b If I _____ (realise) the ice was so thin,

c We _____ (not break) down

d We _____ (sit) somewhere else

e If I _____ (not go) into town that day,

1 if you _____ (have) the car serviced.

2 I _____ (not meet) an old friend.

3 I _____ (not go) skating.

4 if we _____ (be told) the seats were behind a pillar.

5 if he _____ (not be) a great athlete.

KEY WORD TRANSFORMATIONS

> ### » EXAM HELPLINE
>
> **Part 4: Key word transformations**
>
> » Read the second sentence, ignoring the key word, and try to work out how to make the sentences similar in meaning.
>
> » Don't leave out any information in the first sentence.
>
> » Count the number of words you want to insert carefully. Remember that contractions count as two words.
>
> » Items which are often tested include:
>
>   - *for* and *since*
>   - idiomatic expressions
>   - nouns to verbs and verbs to nouns
>   - reported speech
>   - conditionals

9 **For questions 1–8, complete the second sentence so that it has a similar meaning to the first sentence, using the word given. Do not change the word given. You must use between two and five words, including the word given.**

1 'How does everyone feel the meeting went?' Robin asked.

  know

  Robin wanted _____ the meeting had gone.

2 You failed the test because you didn't revise.

  done

  If you _____, you would have passed the test.

3 What do you find appealing about being a sports coach?

  want

  Why _____ a sports coach?

4 Paul joined a band and left his job.

  gave

  Paul _____ join a band.

5 I am not planning to go to university.

  intention

  I _____ to university.

6 Your son's success in the race is something to be proud of.

  must

  You _____ your son's success in the race.

7 Kate began studying French two years ago.

  for

  Kate _____ two years now.

8 You should look after yourself more.

  care

  If you _____, you'd be healthier.

MULTIPLE CHOICE

1 **Look at this photo of a builderer and read questions 1–7. How do you think *builderers* are different to normal climbers?**

1 What does Brian say about builderers?

  A Every serious climber becomes a builderer at some time.

  B Builderers often perform stunts in films like *Spider-Man*.

  C Most climbers find the idea of buildering appealing.

2 Why does Brian think some climbers become builderers?

  A They don't live near enough to any climbing walls.

  B They don't have many places to climb.

  C They need practice before climbing mountains.

3 Brian advises people wanting to climb buildings to

  A inform the owners of the buildings.

  B get mountaineering experience before climbing buildings.

  C try to avoid getting caught.

4 What problems might new climbers have trying to become builderers?

  A They won't be allowed to climb on their own.

  B They might find the height of the buildings terrifying.

  C They might find learning to tie the ropes difficult.

5 If you are determined to become a builderer, Brian suggests that you

  A avoid any publicity for your climb.

  B arrange to climb on a quiet day.

  C join an organisation to get some financial help.

6 What comparison does Brian make between climbing buildings and climbing mountains?

  A None of the equipment used is the same.

  B You need a similar mentality to do both types of climbing.

  C Builderers and other climbers view the climb in different ways.

7 What comment does Brian make about climbing buildings?

  A Glass-fronted skyscrapers are the worst buildings to climb.

  B Some buildings are too well guarded for builderers to climb.

  C Many buildings are far too difficult for builderers to climb.

2 **(◎ 14) You will hear an interview with Brian Abbot, who is a builderer. For questions 1–7, choose the best answer (A, B or C).**

›› EXAM HELPLINE

Part 4: Multiple choice

›› The information in the recording is in the same order as it appears in the questions.

›› Never put more than one letter in each box on the answer sheet. You will lose a mark even if one letter is correct.

Do you think builderers are a danger to the public? Why?/Why not?

Should people who take risks expect others to rescue them when things go wrong? Why?/Why not?

COLLABORATIVE TASK AND DISCUSSION

1 What do you think these photos have in common?

2 Read the exam task and underline the most important words. What questions do you think will appear above the photos in the exam?

Here are some pictures of things that people can do to keep fit and healthy.

First, talk to each other about how successful these things might be in helping people to stay healthy. Then decide which one is the most important for a healthy life.

3 In pairs, do the task in 2 using some of these phrases.

Reaching a decision

Let's make a decision, shall we?

So which one are we going to/shall we choose?

Well, we both seem to agree that ...

Agreeing to disagree

Well, I don't really agree with ...

So we have different opinions about ...

So we can't agree about ...

>> EXAM HELPLINE

Part 4: Discussion

» Try to develop the topic and not just give short answers.

» This is a three-way discussion so you can talk to your partner as well as the examiner.

» If the examiner asks your partner a question directly, don't answer it yourself.

» Remember, you don't have to agree with your partner's opinions – you can agree to have different opinions.

4 In pairs, discuss the questions.

a How can parents encourage their children to lead healthy lives?

b What's your opinion of fast food?

c Do you think sport should be compulsory at school? Why?/Why not?

d Some people say we worry too much about our health nowadays. What's your opinion?

e Do you think it's more interesting to play sport or to watch sport on the television? Why?

f Are all sports equally good for your health? Why?/Why not?

REFLEXIVE PRONOUNS Extension p76 text

1 Reflexive pronouns are used when the object of the verb refers back to the subject, e.g. *ask yourself*. Use these verbs and a reflexive pronoun to complete sentences a–e.

| help | enjoy | teach | blame | introduce |

a The students _____ to the new teacher.
b I don't think I could _____ another language.
c Don't all stand there waiting to be served. _____!
d We are going to _____ on the picnic, whatever the weather.
e Ted _____ for the accident.

VERBS OF MOVEMENT Revision p77 ex3

2 Use the correct form of these verbs to complete sentences a–i. More than one answer may be possible.

creep	fumble	leap
freeze	bound	tiptoe
stare	fling	crouch

a Peter was angry. He _____ his jacket on the bedroom floor.
b It's rude to _____ at people!
c We _____ out of the garden, bending down behind the low wall, afraid that someone would hear us.
d The small child _____ down to stroke the black kitten.
e If we _____ along the corridor without our shoes, no one will be able to hear us.
f The animal ran across the field and _____ across the stream.
g Richard _____ with his keys as he tried to open the car door.
h Suddenly a cat _____ across the road in front of the car.
i Everyone in the safari jeep _____ as the lion walked towards the vehicle.

PHRASAL VERBS WITH SET Revision p77 ex4

3 Use a phrasal verb with set to complete sentences a–e. More than one answer may be possible.

a I think the rain has _____ for the day.
b The problems we had _____ the project _____ by two weeks.
c What time did you _____ from home this morning?
d Could you _____ your ideas on paper?
e How difficult is it to _____ your own business?

USING ADVERBS Extension p78 ex4

4 Choose the best adverb (a, b, c or d) to complete sentences 1–4.

1 The lady sitting opposite me was _____ tall and thin.
   a immediately   c extremely
   b abruptly   d completely
2 Conrad made his excuses and _____ left the dinner table.
   a hurriedly   c hesitantly
   b fully   d hardly
3 'Can I help you?' asked the receptionist. 'No,' replied the man _____.
   a apologetically   c rudely
   b nervously   d kindly
4 'I'd love to stay, but I really do have to go now,' said Bill _____.
   a incredibly   c actually
   b reluctantly   d slightly

ORDER OF ADJECTIVES Revision p78/79 ex5–6

5 Put the words in descriptions a–f in the correct order.

a red a Chinese scarf silk
b suede black coat long a
c man grey a(n) hair with old short
d bracelet cheap-looking a plastic
e watch expensive gold a(n)
f evening cold a November miserable

PHRASES WITH *LOOK* Revision p79 ex7

6 Choose the correct words to complete sentences a–g.

a It's important to eat properly if you want to look *after / over* yourself.

b The flat isn't much to look *back / at*, but we like it.

c I don't like the look *with / of* that hotel. Let's stay somewhere else.

d Nobody over 25 really wants to look their *age / years*, do they?

e If you look *around / after*, you'll see some fantastic buildings.

f After the success of his first film, the director has never looked *back / round*.

g Looking *after / ahead*, I think the company has a great future.

USING CONDITIONALS Revision p80/81 ex4–8

7 Put the verbs in brackets in sentences a–g into the zero, first, second or third conditional.

a If Rosy _____ (not go) to the nightclub, she _____ (not met) her new boyfriend.

b If I _____ (be) a top footballer, I _____ (be) rich and famous.

c Ice _____ (melt) if you _____ (heat) it.

d We _____ (go) for a run tomorrow if the weather _____ (be) fine.

e If I _____ (can) speak English perfectly, I _____ (get) a job as an interpreter.

f If you _____ (mix) the colours red and blue, you _____ (get) purple.

8 Correct the mistakes in sentences a–h.

a If you will arrive early tomorrow, can you open all the windows in the classroom?

b If I am you, I'd discuss the problem with my parents.

c Would you mind if I would ask you a question?

d If I had know the answer to the question, I would have told you.

e If you dropped eggs, the shells break.

f Pete would have been ready earlier if he had spend so long in the shower.

g If you had been driving just a little more slowly, you would stopped at the traffic lights.

h We will can go out if you have finished the work.

9 Complete sentences a–d in your own words.

a If I were running the country, I _____.

b If I have time, I _____.

c It would have been nice if _____.

d If I hadn't been so lazy, I _____.

WRITING Extension p82 listening text

10 Write a paragraph (about 150 words) describing your attitude towards sport. Say

– what sports you are interested in.

– whether you prefer to play or watch them.

– what you do to keep fit.

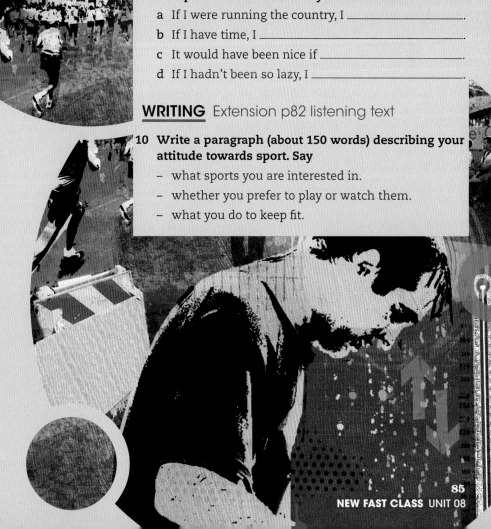

MULTIPLE MATCHING

1 Quickly read the extracts (A–D) from emails sent to a news website and find out what problems the four people are having.

> Do you feel sympathetic towards the people who wrote the emails? Why?/Why not?
>
> What advice would you give the people who wrote the emails?

A How can we resolve this situation?

I am a student and have been sharing a house for six months with four other people. We all get on well, but one issue is causing trouble. It may sound trivial, but one of my housemates keeps piles of dirty plates and cutlery in his room for weeks on end. At times, we have been left with only two clean plates between the five of us. We are
5 reluctant to clean up after him, but he seems incapable of tidying up himself. He never apologises for the inconvenience he causes, claiming that life is harder for him than for us as he failed his previous year at university and is having to repeat it. We have talked to him and written him notes, but nothing works. He is a lovely guy, and we don't want to fall out with him, but he consistently evades his share of
10 household tasks. How can we get him to change his habits?

B How does one rebuild a social existence from nothing?

I've never really been any good at making friends. I was a very withdrawn child and have never really grown out of it. After leaving school I felt I wanted to move on – I didn't want to see people from school again until I had achieved something in my life and proved myself. The same applied when I left university: although I
15 wanted to catch up with friends again, I was afraid of feeling inferior. I have always felt the need to justify myself to people before they will accept me. For one reason or another, I have only ever had short-term, superficial relationships with people. I have always moved on, cutting all ties with the past, and as a result I only have a limited range of social acquaintances. Is it too late to try to change this situation?
20 I don't particularly lack confidence or self-esteem now, merely opportunities to form lasting friendships. How does one rebuild a social existence from nothing?

C How can I deal with this situation?

My younger sister and I are both in our 30s and do not get on. I don't know whether to accept the situation or try to change things. We fought constantly throughout our childhood. She would attack me verbally, and I would respond by retreating
25 into a book and completely ignoring her. Our father chose to spend more time with me, pointing out to her that I was far more like him than she was. After leaving home, I moved to another city and saw my sister only at family gatherings. A few years ago, I suggested going out for a meal to see if we could put the past behind us. She took the opportunity to list a series of events from our teenage years and
30 then left angrily, saying that she didn't want to see me again. I was invited to her wedding a year or so ago, but we spent the whole time avoiding each other. What should I do?

D Should I just give up on this relationship?

In the past nine months, I have become increasingly at odds with my best friend, who is in her first year of university. We used to get on enormously well, but as I've
35 matured, my conversations have turned more to global and political affairs, which I feel passionately about. I'm a very open-minded person, but she has very fixed views about everything. Despite all this, she is a reliable and trustworthy friend. I feel that whereas I form my opinions rationally, she hasn't matured enough to think for herself. As a result, I am reluctant to talk to her at all, for fear of being
40 disagreed with. I avoided seeing her over the holidays, which led to a massive row. I told her that I wasn't going to put up with the way she was treating me, but did not go into details. She told me that I always try to force my opinions on her. We don't share any mutual friends and I believe she will never compromise, so should I just let this friendship go?

Part 3: Multiple matching

» Skim read all the extracts quickly each time you answer a question.

» For each question, make sure the prompt really does match information in the extract you have chosen.

2 **Read the extracts again. For questions 1–15, choose from the extracts (A–D). The extracts may be chosen more than once.**

Which extract mentions someone who

1 had a parent who felt closer to one child than another?

2 feels they have drifted apart from a good friend?

3 was shy as a child?

4 feels their life is more difficult than anyone else's?

5 has difficulty forming lasting relationships?

6 is causing problems because of untidiness?

7 holds different opinions from their friend?

8 reacted to a situation by ignoring the other person?

9 feels more grown-up than their friend?

10 is not prepared to face up to their responsibilities?

11 tried to solve a problem with a member of the family?

12 is tired of a friend's disapproval?

13 felt they weren't as good as their friends?

14 didn't see eye to eye with a family member?

15 refuses to take any notice of criticism?

TALKING ABOUT FEELINGS AND CAPABILITIES

3 **Choose the best meaning (a or b) for the expressions 1–6.**

1 be reluctant to
   a be unwilling to   b be nervous about

2 be incapable of
   a not want to   b not have the ability to

3 be laid back about
   a be relaxed about   b be lazy about

4 be unable to
   a not have the   b not know how to
     inclination to

5 be defensive about something
   a try to avoid criticism   b be confident about

6 have difficulty
   a not find it easy to   b not be happy about

PHRASAL VERBS WITH MORE THAN TWO PARTS

4 **What does *give up on* mean in the title of text D? Underline the phrasal verbs in a–e and match them with the meanings 1–5.**

a I don't want to argue with you but I've run out of patience.

b Sorry, I can't talk now. I'll catch up with you later.

c You'll just have to face up to the fact that you've got responsibilities in your life now.

d I was surprised to hear that Sally's broken up with her boyfriend.

e I think I'm coming down with a cold.

1 become ill

2 get in touch with

3 end a relationship with

4 finish or exhaust

5 accept and deal with something difficult

> What makes you feel fed up?
> How often do you manage to catch up with your friends?

FORMAL TRANSACTIONAL EMAIL

1 Read the exam question and the advert opposite and find out

a what the advert is for.

b what extra information is required.

You have seen this advert in a student newspaper. Read the advert and the notes you have made. Then write an email of 120–150 words to the organisation, using all your notes.

Work for a penfriend agency

Do you fancy earning some <u>extra money</u> working for a new company that finds penfriends for young people in countries all around the world? We aim to provide contacts for those who want to practise a foreign language, make new friends, or arrange exchange holidays. We also guarantee to do our best to match people with similar interests. The job is <u>part-time</u> and you can easily <u>work</u> from home. If you're interested, email us now at the address below and we'll send you an online application form. If your application is successful, you'll be given a <u>telephone interview</u>.

How much?

What kind of work?

Number of hours/ days a week?

When?

2 Read Kelly's email to the penfriend organisation and underline formal words or expressions which mean the same as the informal expressions a–h.

a to answer

b which I saw

c extra

d talk about

e for every hour

f in connection with

g what kind of ... it is?

h happen

FORMAL PHRASES

3 Complete sentences a–g using the words in brackets and ideas of your own.

a I am writing in reply ... (your advert/the university website)

b I am interested in ... (apply/job/penfriend agency)

c I would like ... (additional information/the job)

d Could you tell me ... (hours/would be)?

e Could you let me know ... (salary/would be)?

f I would also like to know ... (when/you interview candidates)

g I look forward to ... (receive/your reply)

Dear Sir/Madam

I am writing in reply to your advertisement, which recently appeared in the Newtown College student newspaper. I am very interested in working for your organisation, but I would like some additional information about what the job would involve.

You mention earning extra money. Could you tell me how much this might be? Would it be paid on a daily or an hourly basis? You also refer to the fact that the job is part-time, but exactly how many hours per week does that mean?

Regarding working from home, could you let me know what form this work would take? I would also like to know when the telephone interview would take place.

I look forward to hearing from you soon.

Yours faithfully

Kelly Dexter

CHECKING YOUR WORK

4 Read Clara's email opposite and find and correct 15 mistakes. There are grammar, lexical, spelling and punctuation mistakes.

WRITING A FORMAL EMAIL

5 You have seen the advert below in a student newspaper. Read the advert and the notes you have made. Then write an email of 120–150 words to the organisation using all your notes.

> **EXAM HELPLINE**

Part 1: Formal transactional email

» You must answer the Part 1 question. It is equally as important as the question in Part 2 so allow enough time for both.

» It is important to know roughly how many words you write, but don't waste time counting them exactly. Estimate the number of words to a line and count the number of lines.

» Use the *Writing guide* on page 117.

Dear Sir/Madam

I am writing for reply to your advertisement about penfriends. I am interesting in write to a penfriend in another country. but I would like some additional information about your organisation.

You mentioning corresponding with people in diferent countries. Could you tell to me which countries you have contacts in! Can I choose the country and the language myself? You also refer the fact that young people can join. However, could you confirm whether you have lower age limit?

Regarding the charge you make for your services, could you let me know when I would have pay this? I could also like to know how long would my membership last.

I look forward of hearing from you soon.

Faithfully

Clara Bernard

HOLIDAY WORK AVAILABLE

Do you fancy <u>working</u> on a summer camp for young people in <u>another country</u>? Whether you're interested in seeing the world or just want to help young people, we will provide you with exciting <u>paid work</u> opportunities in sports coaching, catering and other areas. Simply fill in the <u>application form</u>. We guarantee to do our best to match your interests to the positions available.

Email us now at the address below.

Length of contract?

Which countries?

How much?

Application form not on the website

MULTIPLE-CHOICE CLOZE

1 Read the text quickly, ignoring the gaps, and find out how teams of dogs and their handlers ended up being the symbols of Alaska.

> **» EXAM HELPLINE**
>
> **Part 1: Multiple-choice cloze**
>
> » Read the text quickly for gist.
>
> » Remember that the answers are usually a mixture of letters. If all your answers are, e.g. A, you have probably made some mistakes.

2 For questions 1–12, read the text again and decide which answer (A, B, C or D) best fits each gap.

0 A appeared B reached C came D took
1 A scream B shout C cry D call
2 A outburst B outbreak C output D outlook
3 A but B just C except D simply
4 A expect B rely C wait D depend
5 A resolution B reason C response D result
6 A cut through B cut off C cut out D cut back
7 A means B course C variety D style
8 A directed B transmitted C sent D posted
9 A picked B heaped C gathered D collected
10 A Faced B Met C Opposed D Dealt
11 A travel B trip C voyage D tour
12 A grown B developed C become D got

How teamwork saved Alaska

Winner First Place.

Col. Ramsay's Entry, 3rd All Alaska Sweepstakes, John Johnson, Driver.

Many years ago, dogsleds ⁰_____ to the rescue of Alaskans in a marathon of life and death. On a cold January day in 1925, Dr Curtis Welch sent out a ¹_____ for help through the network of telegraph and radio stations. Medicine was urgently needed for an ²_____ of diphtheria in the remote town of Nome. A small amount of medicine was available in Anchorage, ³_____ it was not enough for the whole population, and most of Nome's citizens had to ⁴_____ for more to be sent from Seattle.

At the turn of the last century, Nome was a growing town of several thousand people which had come into existence as a ⁵_____ of the gold rush. The harbour town, which is just below the Arctic Circle, became ⁶_____ every autumn when ice formed over the Bering Sea. The only ⁷_____ of transport to the outside world in those days was by dog team.

The medicine was first ⁸_____ by rail to the end of the line, 1,100km from Nome. From there it was ⁹_____ and transported by relays of courageous dog handlers. ¹⁰_____ with winter darkness, a merciless gale and brutal temperatures of –50°C, some handlers probably wished they'd never embarked on such a mission. Nevertheless, they completed the exhausting ¹¹_____ in five and a half days. The epidemic was broken and the quarantine lifted. Since then, the dogs and their handlers have ¹²_____ the symbols of Alaska.

Correct any of the sentences a–f which are incorrect.

a I wish I would be able to speak English perfectly.

b I wish my brother would stop playing loud music late at night.

c We regret informing you that you have not been successful in your application.

d Paul wishes he were good at sports.

e We wish we have never gone on that holiday.

f I don't regret to choose this job.

REGRET (DOING)/REGRET (TO DO)

3 **What is the difference between** *I regret saying* **and** *I regret to say***? Rewrite sentences a–f using** *regret (doing)* **or** *regret (to do)***.**

a We're sorry to tell you that the wedding has been cancelled.

b Lucy isn't sorry she took up nursing.

c My aunt isn't sorry that she gave up smoking.

d I'm sorry, but I have to say that I don't think this relationship is working out.

e My best friend isn't sorry that she split up with her boyfriend.

f We have to inform you that the 8.30 train has been delayed by 40 minutes.

EXPRESSING WISHES ABOUT THE PAST

4 **Find a sentence in the text in 1 with** *wished***. What tense is used after** *wished***? Match these sentences with meanings a–b.**

> I wish I had never bought the dress.
>
> I wish I had bought the dress.

a I didn't do this but I now regret it.

b I did this but I now regret it.

5 **Express the main idea in sentences a–e using the words in brackets. More than one answer may be possible.**

a My parents took us to that new restaurant and it was terrible. (if only)

b My grandparents have never been abroad. (wish)

c We moved house six months ago, and now I can't see my old friends. (if only)

d Sam doesn't like the pink colour his mother chose for his bedroom walls. (wish)

e The second-hand car that he bought is always breaking down. (if only)

EXPRESSING WISHES ABOUT THE PRESENT AND THE FUTURE

6 **Use these words to complete sentences a–d.**

wasn't	would	didn't	could

a I wish Ted _____ stop playing that music so loud, but he won't.

b I wish I _____ afford to go on holiday, but I can't.

c I wish my father _____ have to work so hard, but he does.

d I wish Harry _____ going to study abroad, but he is.

7 **Add short sentences to a–d using** *wish* **and either** *would/wouldn't* **or a verb in the past simple. More than one answer may be possible.**

I can't speak Japanese. *I wish I could say a few words.*

My son never tidies his room. *I wish he would tidy his room.*

a George doesn't get on very well with his brother. He _____.

b My friends are always sending me junk emails. I _____.

c Susan never remembers Jack's birthday. He _____ _____.

d Paul hasn't got a girlfriend. He _____ _____.

SENTENCE COMPLETION

1 Read the questions in the exam task below and decide what parts of speech the missing words might be.

2 (○15) You will hear a dancer, Giovanna Mendes, talking about her life and work. For questions 1–10, complete the sentences.

3 Were your predictions in 1 correct?

> What impression do you think Giovanna gives of the life of a professional dancer?

Giovanna Mendes
Dancer

Giovanna's favourite treat is ¹_____.

Giovanna was born on the ²_____ 1979.

Her mother works as a ³_____.

Giovanna found school ⁴_____.

Her most exciting time was when she joined the ⁵_____, aged 13.

People in ⁶_____ are often her biggest critics.

Giovanna gives her best performances when doing ⁷_____ dancing.

She finds ⁸_____ the best way to relax.

Giovanna says that she is ⁹_____ in her work.

She would like to ¹⁰_____ some time in the future.

» EXAM HELPLINE

Part 2: Sentence completion

» Check that your answers fit the sentence grammatically.

» Although correct spelling is not absolutely essential, the words in your answer must closely resemble the words you hear.

» Many of the answers you need may be just one word.

SPELLING: THE *SCHWA* /ə/ SOUND

4 (○16) The word *performance* has three syllables (*per/form/ance*), but the first syllable is not stressed and the vowel is pronounced /ə/. Listen and write the words from the text that contain the /ə/ sound.

a _____   d _____

b _____   e _____

c _____   f _____

THE LONG TURN

1 Use the sentence openers to explain the meaning of both words in brackets.

  a (a nightclub / a café)

    A … is a place where you go to …

  b (elderly people / grandparents)

    They're people who …

  c (friendship / relationship)

    A … is when you …

  d (youngsters / teenagers)

    … means … , but … means …

2 Which words from 1 would you use to describe the situations in the photos? Which tense would you use to describe the photos?

3 In pairs, take it in turns to compare one pair of photos and say how important you think the relationships are to the people. Use these words to help you.

think	seem	look like
appear to be	imagine	look as if

» EXAM HELPLINE

Part 2: The long turn

» Use appropriate tenses when doing the task.

» Don't worry if you don't know or can't remember a word – just paraphrase.

---

4 Correct the mistakes in sentences a–i.

  a The friendship is very important for young people.

  b These friends seem to be getting well with each other.

  c The dancers are enjoying more than the other people.

  d The elderly people look like happy.

  e I don't think these people are as close than the ones in the first picture.

  f Everybody likes spend a time with their friends.

  g We must to look after elderly people.

  h This relationship it seems more closer than the one in the second picture.

  i The men, they sit in a café.

REFLEXIVE PRONOUNS AS EMPHASISERS

Extension p86 text

1 We can use reflexive pronouns to emphasise that someone did something on their own or without help. Use a suitable pronoun to complete sentences a–e.

Example: Dan built the garage *himself*.

a I wrote this poem _____.

b If we can't find anyone to decorate our house, we'll have to paint it _____.

c Our toddler Anna can switch on the TV by _____.

d Did you know that DIY means Do-it-_____.

e The children will have to cook dinner _____ tonight.

PHRASAL VERBS WITH *FALL*

Extension p86 text

2 Match the phrasal verbs in sentences a–f with meanings 1–6.

a Our neighbours haven't spoken to us since we *fell out* two years ago.

b If we spend all our money, we'll have nothing to *fall back on* in an emergency.

c We'd made lots of plans for the weekend, but they all *fell through*.

d The team members disagreed about how to celebrate their win, but everyone was eventually happy to *fall in with* the coach's plans.

e Pat and Martin *fell for* each other when they first met.

f We must buy some new furniture – these old chairs are *falling apart*!

1 agree to

2 have a disagreement

3 be attracted to

4 not succeed

5 break into pieces

6 rely on for support

3 Use the correct form of the phrasal verbs in 2 to complete sentences a–f.

a Despite some disagreement, everyone eventually _____ our idea to go to the cinema.

b I need a new bike. This one is so old, it's _____!

c I'm afraid to say that Sue and I _____ last year and we aren't speaking now.

d What will we _____ if we lose our jobs?

e Unfortunately, our plans to go to America _____ at the last minute.

f Do you think you can _____ someone the moment you meet them?

EXPRESSIONS WITH *PUT* Extension p86 text

4 Match the expressions with *put* in sentences a–e with meanings 1–5.

a I'm not going to *put up with* any more of your complaints!

b Please don't *put me off* when I'm trying to concentrate on my homework.

c I think Sally was a bit *put out* when I said I couldn't come to her party.

d Sam's going to *put in for* a transfer to another branch of the company.

e I don't like Kelly – she's always trying to *put people down*.

1 distract or disturb

2 apply formally for

3 tolerate

4 make someone appear silly or stupid

5 upset or disappointed

WRITING Extension p86 text

5 Write a paragraph (about 150 words) about a person who has had a great influence on your life. Say

– who they are.

– why they have had such a great influence on your life.

– how you feel about them.

PHRASAL VERBS WITH MORE THAN TWO PARTS Revision p87 ex4

6 Use the correct form of these phrasal verbs to complete sentences a–e.

| catch up with | face up to | come down with |
| break up with | run out of | |

a My brother is really ill. He _____ with a bad cold.

b I won't finish the exam. I've _____ time.

c Diana will have to _____ the fact that she has to earn her own living now.

d I'm so busy these days that I just don't have time to _____ my friends.

e Suzie's really sad. She _____ her boyfriend.

EXPRESSIONS CONNECTED WITH WORK

Extension p88 ex1

7 Match the expressions connected with work in a–g with their opposites in 1–7.

a earn a good salary

b do part-time work

c be self-employed

d commute to work

e do a temporary job

f apply for a job

g work long hours

1 be employed by (someone else)

2 resign from a job

3 be underpaid

4 have a permanent job

5 work nine to five

6 work from home

7 have a full-time job

I WISH Revision p91 ex4–7

8 Make wishes about the past, present and future using the information in sentences a–i, beginning *I wish*.

a I forgot to do my homework last night.

b I can't afford to go to the disco tomorrow night.

c I haven't got time to watch the film on TV.

d I didn't go to Sue's party. Apparently everyone had a great time.

e I'm not very good at sport.

f My best friend is going to move to another town.

g Toby always borrows my things. I don't like it.

h The shoes which I bought are really uncomfortable.

i I'd like to play a musical instrument, but I can't.

I WISH AND *IF ONLY* Extension p91 ex4–7

9 Put the verbs in brackets into the correct form in sentences a–f. More than one answer may be possible.

a I wish you _____ (stop) interrupting me!

b If only I _____ (not have to) go to school today.

c I wish I _____ (can) speak English perfectly.

d If only I _____ (listen) to what the teacher said in class yesterday.

e I wish you _____ (come) to the party tomorrow night.

f Jill wishes she _____ (study) more last term.

INFINITIVES, *-ING* AND MEANING

Extension p92 Listening text

10 Match the verbs in sentences a–d with meanings 1–4.

a I always remember to lock the door when I go out.

b I tried to understand what the maths teacher was saying, but I couldn't.

c I tried turning the key in the lock gently, but it wouldn't open.

d I remember playing with my friends when I was a child.

1 It wasn't possible for me to do something.

2 I did something which I still remember.

3 I remember something, then do it.

4 I did something but it wasn't successful.

11 Complete sentences a–e with *remember*, *regret* or *try* and the correct form of the verbs in brackets.

a _____ (read) through your work when you finish writing an essay.

b Can you be quiet? I _____ (work).

c I _____ (move) here. I hate this town!

d Please _____ (post) my letter when you go out.

e I _____ (turn) the switch, but it didn't start.

MULTIPLE CHOICE

1 Answer the questions

a What kind of art do you like: modern or traditional?

b Do you think it's usually difficult to make a lot of money as an artist? Why?/Why not?

2 Quickly read the article and find out how the Chinese art world is changing.

> Do you think artists should be idealistic and not worry about money? Why?/Why not?
>
> Do you think it's a bad thing to become successful very early in life? Why?/Why not?

On a recent lazy afternoon, Wang Haiyang, a student at China's top art school, was quietly packing away some of his new oil paintings in the campus' printmaking department. He is 23, and he has just had his first major art exhibition at a big Beijing gallery. Many of his works sold for more than $3,000 each, and he hasn't even graduated! 'This is one of my new works,' he said proudly, gesturing towards a painting of a couple. 'I'll be having another show in Singapore in March.'

Beijing's state-run Central Academy of Fine Arts has been transformed into a breeding ground for hot young artists and designers who are quickly snapped up by dealers in Beijing and Shanghai. The school is so selective that it turns away more than 90 percent of its applicants each year. Many of its faculty members are millionaires. And with the booming demand for contemporary Chinese art, its students are suddenly so popular that collectors frequently show up on campus in search of the next art superstar. At the annual students' exhibition, the students no longer label their works only with their name and a title. They leave an email address and mobile phone number.

'I can say that we have the best students and the best faculty in China,' said Zhu Di, the school's admissions director. 'And we give students a bright future.' Yet as the academy reshapes its campus, its flowering relationship with the art market is creating unease among those who feel that students should be shielded from commercial pressures. 'The buyers are going to the school to look for the next superstar,' said Cheng Xindong, a dealer in Beijing. 'And immediately they make contact with them, they say "I will buy everything from you." This can be a dangerous thing. These young artists need time to develop.'

In the 1980s, the school occupied a modest plot of land in central Beijing and had about 200 students. Today, the school has a new 33-acre campus and more than 2,000 students. It offers majors in design and architecture and courses in digital and video art, and some of its graduates are making millions. 'In the old days,' Zhu Di said, 'students had a passion for art. They viewed art as a way of life. Now, as society has changed, more and more students view art as a job. Students are more practical.'

The new campus, which is about 10 miles north of its former site, has trendy cafés, attractive dining facilities, spacious classrooms and art studios and sophisticated equipment. Faculty salaries are low, but pay means little to most of these teachers, whose canvases might as well be painted in gold. Sui Jianguo, the school's dean and one of the country's most acclaimed sculptors, has seen his works sell for as much as $150,000. The prestige of teaching at the nation's most elite art school remains a major draw for such artists.

Some faculty members at the Central Academy do privately regret the decline of traditional Chinese painting and disciplined training in centuries-old mediums. And some complained that today's art students are not as idealistic as they used to be. But other teachers said that their students, largely born in the 1980s, simply reflect the changes sweeping China, which have brought about more prosperous conditions in the country and given it more global awareness.

Most of the faculty agrees on one major shift: present-day students seem less interested in what is going on around them and more concerned about their personal struggles and issues of identity. Wang Haiyang, who will graduate this year, paints canvases depicting someone who looks very much like himself: short, with large, expressive eyes. 'They tell my own story – my mentality,' he said of his works. 'The whole process of art is like a process to cure myself.'

YOUNG ARTISTS WELL SCHOOLED IN MARKET FORCES

3 **Read the article again. For questions 1–8, choose the answer (A, B, C or D) which you think fits best according to the text.**

1 What does the writer suggest about Wang Haiyang in the first paragraph?

A He has been having a rather lazy time recently.

B He has just finished doing a university degree.

C He has just had a very successful exhibition of his work.

D He has sold a painting to a couple who came to his exhibition.

2 The writer uses the phrase 'snapped up' in line 12 to show that the young artists

A are all in very great demand.

B compete fiercely against each other.

C contact dealers immediately on entering college.

D become angry if art dealers do not contact them.

3 Why do students leave their email and phone number at the annual exhibition?

A This is how they make new friends.

B This is the only way they can contact members of the public.

C They are expecting to be contacted by collectors.

D This is the only form of advertising they are allowed to do.

4 What does the writer highlight about the Central Academy's students in paragraph 3?

A the delight of everyone at the school's success

B a disadvantage of becoming successful too quickly

C the difficulty of surviving financially as an artist

D the range of opportunities open to talented artists

5 What is suggested about the Central Academy in paragraph 4?

A It has grown too big too quickly.

B It places too much emphasis on technology.

C Its students have become disillusioned with the art world.

D Its students have different motives for becoming artists nowadays.

6 What comment does the writer make about the school's teachers in paragraph 5?

A Few people can afford to purchase the teachers' works of art.

B Teachers have no difficulty obtaining large sums for their work.

C Teachers are not motivated by money earned from their works of art.

D Low salaries can cause real financial problems for teaching staff.

7 Some faculty members feel that the students

A are rather materialistic in their attitude towards life.

B are far too traditional in their approach to work.

C express their country's new image in the works they produce.

D produce work which often seems to be lacking in imagination.

8 What do most faculty members agree about?

A Students are more interested then ever in their surroundings.

B Students are too concerned about what is going on in the world.

C Students sometimes find it very difficult to form relationships.

D Students are more worried about who they are.

PHRASAL VERBS WITH *TURN*

4 **What does *turns away* in lines 13–14 of the text mean? Choose the correct meaning (a or b) of the phrasal verbs in sentences 1–6.**

1 We decided to drive into town to see a film, but it began to snow so heavily that we had to *turn back*.

a take another route

b return to the place you started

2 Brad was offered the job, but in the end he decided to *turn it down*.

a not to accept   b exchange for another

3 Our weekend break by the sea *turned into* a bit of a nightmare.

a become   b produce

4 Can you *turn* the television *down*, please?

a switch off   b reduce the sound of

5 They took the old painting to an art dealer, and it *turned out* to be worth a lot of money.

a be discovered   b surprise

6 If you *turn* the book *over*, you'll see the author's picture on the back.

a open   b look at the other side of

INFORMAL TRANSACTIONAL LETTER

1 **Read the exam question, the advertisement below and the notes, and correct any false information in sentences a–e.**

a The digital camera is new.

b The camera is in good condition.

c The camera didn't come with a memory card.

d Part of the camera bag is missing.

e The camera is worth more than £120.

You have seen this advert on a college noticeboard. Read the advert and the notes you have made. Then write a letter of 120–150 words to the person who wrote the advert, using all your notes.

FOR SALE
digital camera

Anyone interested in buying a second-hand digital camera? Now's your chance! My 10m pixel digital SLR camera is in excellent condition and comes with a 2GB <u>memory card</u>, two extra 18–70mm and 18–105mm <u>zoom lenses</u> and a useful leather <u>camera bag</u>. All for the give-away price of £120!

Write to
Tom Davy, 7 College Road, Shipton, Newcastle NE44

not worth £120

one lens is damaged

no memory card

strap missing

2 **Read Sally's letter to Tom, ignoring the missing words. Has she included all the information in the notes she made on the advertisement?**

Dear Tom

Thanks for the camera I ¹_____ from you this morning. However, I'm sorry to say that after opening the parcel, I was very ²_____ because the equipment that came with the camera was very different from the ³_____ you gave in the advert.

There was no memory card, as you had ⁴_____. There are two extra lenses, but the 18–105mm one is coming apart so it can't be used. As ⁵_____ as the damaged lens, there was no strap for the camera bag, and this will ⁶_____ it very difficult to carry.

⁷_____, I certainly don't feel that £120 was a 'give-away price'. I honestly feel that I've bought something that was overpriced. I'd like to change my mind and return the camera to you, and ask for a ⁸_____.

Hoping to hear from you soon.

Yours

Sally Carter

3 **Choose the best answer, (A, B, C or D) to complete gaps 1–8 in Sally's letter.**

1 A accepted B received C obtained D secured
2 A disapproved B disinterested C disappointed D disagreed
3 A description B detail C report D account
4 A held B told C given D promised
5 A good B well C much D far
6 A make B find C produce D bring
7 A Anything B Anywhere C Anyway D Anyone
8 A restoration B refund C return D receipt

BEFORE, AFTER, WHEN, WHILE + -ING

4 Instead of using tenses, you can use *before, after, when, while* + *-ing*. Use one of the expressions and these verbs to complete sentences a–g. More than one answer may be possible.

cross	book	paint	arrive
finish	travel	have	

a _____ lunch, we went for a walk.

b _____ your tickets, you should ask for a reserved seat.

c _____ in Australia, we met some interesting people.

d _____ at the airport, we realised we'd forgotten our passports.

e _____ the road, remember to look both ways.

f _____ university, I travelled around the world for a year.

g _____ the final picture, he drew a lot of sketches.

PHRASAL VERBS WITH COME

5 What does *coming apart* mean in the letter in 2? Match the phrasal verbs in sentences a–e with the meanings 1–5.

a How did the accident *come about*?

b I *came up with* a great idea for a new sculpture.

c I *came across* a really interesting article about Chinese art in the newspaper.

d The cost of computers is *coming down* all the time.

e The architects *came up against* a lot of problems when they were building the new stadium.

1 be reduced (in value or amount)

2 think of

3 be faced with

4 find or meet by chance

5 happen

EXPRESSIONS WITH CHANGE

6 Use these words to complete the expressions with *change* in sentences a–e.

mind	money	subject	clothes	buses

a We were told we'd have to change _____ in London.

b You can't change your _____ about going on holiday now. I've already booked the hotel.

c Please don't change the _____. We need to discuss this now.

d Could you change this _____ into euros, please?

e I'd like to change my _____ before going out.

> How often do you change your clothes during the day, and why?
> Do you often change your mind?
> When might it be a good idea to change the subject?

WRITING AN INFORMAL LETTER OF COMPLAINT

7 Imagine you have bought something you saw advertised in a local shop window and are not satisfied with it. Write a letter of complaint of 120–150 words. Think of four things you were not satisfied with.

> **» EXAM HELPLINE**
>
> Part 1: Informal transactional letter
>
> » Use a different paragraph for each new idea.
> » Proof read your work carefully for sense and errors.
> » Use the *Writing guide* on page 116.

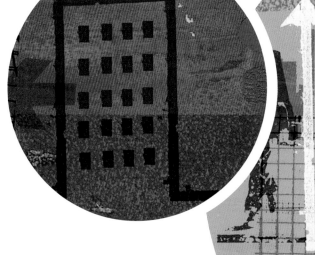

WORD FORMATION

1 Discuss the questions.

a When you buy something, do you ever worry about the effect it might have on the environment?

b Do you think people should worry about this? Why?/Why not?

2 Read the text, ignoring the gaps and the words in capitals. How does the production of pencils and pens affect the environment?

PENCILS, PENS AND PLANET EARTH

Pencils are considered to be one of the most
[0] worthwhile inventions in human history, but when you pick up a pencil, do you ever think about how
[1]_____ the manufacture of these things can be to the environment? Well, perhaps you should.

WORTH

DAMAGE

Pencils are [2]_____ from wood and graphite, but the graphite comes from mines which often pollute local rivers. In terms of the amount of
[3]_____ damage it causes, mining a ton of graphite is much less [4]_____ than the extraction of many other resources from the ground, but think of the millions of people in the world who use pencils!

PRODUCT

ENVIRONMENT

HARM

Some people think that using pens is less
[5]_____ for the environment because pens last longer. With a single biro, you could draw a
[6]_____ line for two miles! A pencil's lead would run out long before that. However, pens aren't a [7]_____ clean alternative. Cheap,
[8]_____ pens are made from plastics, and these come from the oil industry. [9]_____ they also use up large quantities of metal and inks.

DESTROY

CONTINUE

COMPLETE

DISPOSE

FORTUNATE

In the end, we need both pens and pencils. So instead of [10]_____ about which is better for the environment, perhaps we should buy ones which are made from recycled materials.

WORRY

3 Read the text again. Use the word given in capitals at the end of some of the lines to form a word that fits in the gap in the same line.

» EXAM HELPLINE

Part 3: Word formation

» You may need to add another word (as in the example, 0, above) to form the word that fits the gap, e.g. *rain + drop = raindrop*.

» Remember that you will lose a mark if your spelling is incorrect.

TEST YOUR KNOWLEDGE: RELATIVE CLAUSES

Correct any incorrect sentences in a–f using a suitable relative pronoun. In which two sentences can you leave the relative pronoun out? Why?

a This is the book which I was talking about yesterday.

b To who am I speaking?

c The arts festival, that is held every year, is world-famous.

d Maria is the art student whom work won first prize in the exhibition.

e That's the boy which I told you about.

f The footballers which are taking part in the match are all amateurs.

DEFINING OR NON-DEFINING RELATIVE CLAUSES?

4 Which sentence gives us extra information about a fashion show already mentioned? Which sentence tells us which fashion show is a popular event? In which relative clause can you use *that* instead of *which*?

a The fashion show which takes place in Rome is a popular event.

b The fashion show, which takes place in Rome, is a popular event.

USING DEFINING RELATIVE CLAUSES

5 Match the sentence halves using a suitable relative pronoun.

a The villages on either side of the river are joined by a bridge

b Peter Rowlands is the reporter

c This is a statue of the man

d On your right, you can see the square

1 _____ invented the light bulb.

2 _____ was built by the Romans.

3 _____ articles appear in the Sunday papers.

4 _____ the weekly market is still held.

USING NON-DEFINING RELATIVE CLAUSES

6 Use the words in brackets and a suitable relative pronoun to complete the sentences with non-defining relative clauses.

Example:

The first internal combustion engine, (used gas for fuel), was built in 1860 by Etienne Lenoir.

The first internal combustion engine, which used gas for fuel, was built in 1860 by Etienne Lenoir.

a The compass, (originally made in China), was invented thousands of years ago.

b Michael Faraday, (created first electric dynamo for motors), changed our way of life forever.

c Printing machines, (appeared in Europe in about 1440), meant that people could exchange ideas more easily.

d Benjamin Franklin, (experiments taught us a lot about electricity), was a scientist and a politician.

7 Combine sentences a–e and 1–5 with a suitable relative pronoun to make sentences containing non-defining relative clauses.

a The island was discovered only a few years ago.

b The President is visiting Russia.

c The castle is an important historical monument.

d The organisation is helping to reduce pollution in city centres.

e The painter Henri Rousseau lived in Paris for most of his life.

1 It was built in the 17th century.

2 It is situated in the Pacific Ocean.

3 His work can be seen in a new exhibition.

4 His private plane left this morning.

5 It was set up 20 years ago.

MULTIPLE MATCHING

1 Discuss the questions.

a What kinds of things do you enjoy shopping for?

b Do you like to hear background music when you shop? Why?/Why not?

c Do you like to shop alone or go shopping with someone else?

d Do you ever buy clothes with brand names? If so, which brands?

e Which do you think is more important: the quality or the price of an item?

» EXAM HELPLINE

Part 3: Multiple matching

» Read through all the options quickly as you listen to each extract.

» Listen for information expressed in different words.

2 (○ 17) You will hear five different people talking about shopping. Choose from the list (A–F) how each person feels about shopping. Use the letters once only. There is one extra letter which you do not need to use.

A If I have to shop, I prefer to do it on my own.

B I enjoy listening to background music when I shop.

C I couldn't imagine life without going shopping.

D I tend to waste money when I go shopping.

E When I shop I forget all about my worries.

F I get impatient if I have to wait when I shop.

Speaker 1	
Speaker 2	
Speaker 3	
Speaker 4	
Speaker 5	

WORDS CONNECTED WITH BUYING AND SELLING

3 Match a–g with their opposite meanings 1–9. Which word has three opposite meanings?

a spend

b buyers

c consumers

d income

e sales

f increase

g demand

1 expenditure

2 supply

3 suppliers

4 decrease

5 producers

6 save

7 sellers

8 purchases

9 manufacturers

4 Complete sentences a–f with words from 3. More than one answer may be possible.

a We are pleased to announce a huge _____ in the amount of goods sold this year.

b I've managed to _____ enough money to go on holiday this year.

c _____ have the right to return merchandise if it is faulty.

d There is no longer any _____ for this type of mobile phone.

e The artist was unable to _____ us with the canvases we wanted.

f Book _____ often stock excellent quality art books at reasonable prices.

COLLABORATIVE TASK AND DISCUSSION (A GROUP OF THREE)

1 Put the inventions in the photos in the order in which you think they were invented, beginning with the oldest. If you were given these photos in the exam, what do you think the examiner might ask you to talk about?

2 Read the Part 3 exam task and underline the most important words.

Here are some pictures of important inventions.

First, talk to each other about how these inventions have changed our lives. Then decide which two inventions have had the greatest effect on our lives. (4 minutes for groups of three)

3 In groups of three, do the exam task in 2 in the time allowed. Use the photos and some of these phrases.

Inviting both partners to speak

What do you both think about … ?

Have either of you anything else to say about … ?

What about you two? What do you think?

Interrupting politely

Actually, I'd just like to say …

Sorry to interrupt, but …

Could I just say that … ?

» EXAM HELPLINE

Part 3: Collaborative task (a group of three)

» In a group of three, remember to talk to both of the other candidates, not just the same one all the time.

» There will be times when the others are talking and you are silent. If this goes on for too long, think of something to say and interrupt your partners politely.

4 Discuss the questions.

a What other modern inventions have changed the way we live?

b What new thing would you like to invent if you could?

c Do you think technology has made us any happier?

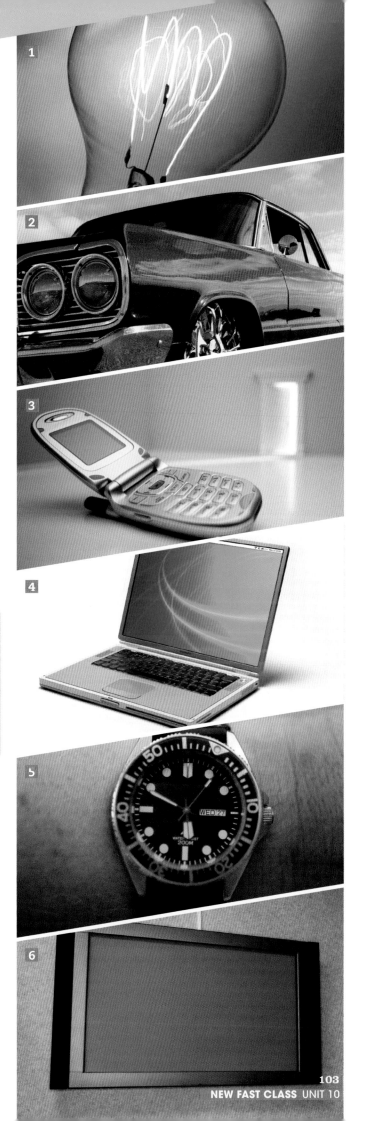

VERBS AND PREPOSITIONS

Extension p96 text

1 Use the prepositions to complete sentences a–d.

to	for	into	on

a I don't like spending money _____ designer clothes.

b He sells his work _____ thousands of dollars.

c Does this style of trainer appeal _____ you?

d The company decided to branch out _____ the art market.

WORDS CONNECTED WITH BUYING AND SELLING Extension p96 text

2 Match these words with the meanings a–h. Then use them to complete sentences 1–8.

priceless	worthless	a bargain	a rip-off
earnings	goods	a rise	cash

a salary

b an increase

c bank notes and coins

d something sold at less than its market price

e having no value or use

f something that costs more than it ought to

g products

h of great value

1 I asked my boss for _____, but she refused to give me one.

2 I bought some designer shoes for $20 dollars – they were such _____!

3 Be careful you don't drop that vase. It's absolutely _____.

4 Surely you didn't pay that much money for a watch like that? What _____!

5 I thought my old computer might fetch some money, but it turned out to be _____.

6 Sam's _____ for the year weren't enough to pay for a family holiday.

7 I'm afraid we only accept _____, not credit cards.

8 A full refund will be given if any _____ are found to be defective.

PHRASAL VERBS WITH *BRING*

Extension p96 text

3 Match the phrasal verbs in italics in a–h with the meanings 1–8.

a Why did he *bring up* that embarrassing incident again in his speech?

b Thanks for lending me the book. I'll *bring* it *back* on Monday.

c I didn't think it would work, but we managed to *bring it off* in the end.

d The financial crisis was *brought about* by irresponsible politicians.

e The failure of their economic policy *brought down* the government.

f The council has *brought in* a tax on rubbish collections.

g I'm afraid we've had to *bring* the meeting *forward* to next week.

h This fashion house is *bringing out* a new style of clothing.

1 defeat or cause the end of something

2 produce

3 return something to someone

4 introduce (a new law)

5 cause to happen

6 move to an earlier date

7 mention in conversation

8 succeed against all expectations

PHRASAL VERBS WITH *TURN* Revision p97 ex4

4 Complete sentences a–f with phrasal verbs with *turn*.

a We'll have to _____ because the snow is too deep.

b It _____ that we had lived next door to each other as children.

c I decided to _____ the job offer in the end.

d If you _____ the page, you will see the exercise I am talking about.

e Tadpoles eventually _____ frogs.

f Can you _____ the TV? I can't hear myself think.

5 Answer questions a–d using phrasal verbs with *turn*.

a What would you say if someone was playing music very loudly?

b Why might you decide not to accept a job offer?

c Is it possible for aggressive children to become nice adults?

d Besides bad weather, why might you stop a journey and go back home?

WRITING Extension p98/99

6 Write a short email to a shop complaining about the poor service you experienced there when you bought an item of clothing. Say

– what happened in the shop.

– why you were not happy with the service.

– how you think the service could be improved.

DEFINING RELATIVE CLAUSES

Revision p101 ex5

7 Complete sentences a–f using the defining relative clauses 1–6 and a suitable relative pronoun. In which sentences can the relative pronoun be left out?

a The film _____ last night was incredibly funny.

b The restaurant _____ turned out to be cheaper than we had expected.

c The sightseeing tour _____ was rather boring.

d The guide _____ was a qualified historian.

e The street _____ was very noisy.

f The nurse _____ was really nice.

1 we went on

2 we stayed on

3 we saw

4 treated me

5 showed us round

6 we had a meal in

8 In which of sentences a–e can you leave out the relative pronoun?

a This is the book that I recommended you should read.

b The man that came to pick me up from the airport was my uncle.

c The dictionary which you borrowed belongs to Maria.

d This is the street that I lived in when I was at university.

e I know a woman who writes detective stories.

NON-DEFINING RELATIVE CLAUSES

Revision p101 ex6–7

9 Combine the sentences in a–g using non-defining relative clauses and suitable relative pronouns. More than one answer may be possible.

a Beth is a very clever person. She's from Wales.

Beth, _____.

b His art exhibition was in the city museum. It was amazing.

His art exhibition, _____.

c The tour guide showed us round the castle. She was a historian.

The tour guide, _____.

d The film was about Christopher Columbus. It lasted three hours.

The film, _____.

e My penfriend is a good sculptor. She lives in France.

My penfriend, _____.

f The town is by the sea. It is famous for its art museums and galleries.

The town, _____.

g This painting is by Umberto Boccioni. It's called *The City Rises*.

This painting, _____.

SPEAKING INDEX

UNIT 02 THE LONG TURN p23 ex4

Which job would you prefer to do?

UNIT 3 COLLABORATIVE TASK p33 ex2

Examiner

Now, I'd like you to talk about something together for about three minutes.

Here are some pictures of things that can make people happy.

First, talk to each other about how these things can make people happy. Then decide which two things bring the most happiness.

›› Questions that would be printed on the paper ‹‹

How can these things make people happy?

Which two things bring the most happiness?

UNIT 5 COLLABORATIVE TASK p53 ex2

Examiner

Now, I'd like you to talk together for about three minutes. I'm just going to listen. I'd like you to imagine that you are choosing two photographs to go on the cover of a book called 'The World in Danger'. Here are some photographs to choose from. First, talk to each other about why the situations in these photographs are dangerous for the world. Then decide which two photographs should go on the cover of the book.

UNIT 07 THE LONG TURN p73 ex2

Examiner

The photographs show different ways of travelling.

I'd like you to compare the photographs and say which way of travelling you think is better.

UNIT 02 THE LONG TURN p23 ex4

Which job do you think looks more interesting?

UNIT 3 DISCUSSION ⊙ 6 p33 ex4

Examiner

What other kinds of things can make people happy?

Candidate 1

Er … I don't know. Lots of things can make people happy or sad.

Examiner

What other kinds of things can make people happy?

Candidate 2

Other kinds of things? … Well … I think … er … maybe being famous … and success too. That can make people happy. Perhaps passing an exam … or getting good marks at school. I know that I feel happy when I do well at school.

UNIT 5 DISCUSSION p53 ex5

1 What can we do to prevent certain kinds of animals dying out?
2 Where do you think airports should be built?
3 Some people say we should stop traffic from driving into city centres. Do you agree?
4 Instead of throwing things away, what could we do with them?
5 How can the countries of the world help each other?
6 Do you think one day human beings might go and live on another planet? Why?

UNIT 07 THE LONG TURN p73 ex7

Examiner (question to listening candidate)

Which of these ways of travelling do you prefer?

GRAMMAR REFERENCE

UNIT 01 *CAN YOU TELL ME …?* p9

The word order in questions of this type is reversed to subject + verb (not verb + subject).

'Are you coming by train?'
Could you let me know if you are coming by train?

'Where is the station?'
Could you tell me where the station is?

UNIT 01 MODALS p11

1 can/could are used:

a to say that someone knows how to do something.
Sam could speak two languages when he was only six years old.

b to make a polite request.
Could/Can you help me with this suitcase?

c to make a suggestion.
We could/can meet for a coffee tomorrow if you like.

d to ask for permission informally.
Could/Can I use your phone?

e to talk about a possibility.
What Teresa said could be true.

f to talk about something it might be possible for you to do.
Can you meet me at the station?

2 be able to is used:

a to say that someone knows how to do something.
Tina is able to fly an aeroplane.

b to talk about something it might be possible for you to do.
Are you able to come to the party tomorrow night?

3 must be/have been, can't be/have been are used:

a to say you are certain that something is true.
Simon must be tired after running in the marathon.
Matt must have been exhausted after all that hard work last week.

b to say that you are certain that something is not true.
Claudia can't be Tim's new girlfriend. She's going out with me!
Celia can't have been at home last night. No one answered when I phoned.

4 must/mustn't are used:

a to say that it is important (not) to do something.
I must remember to post that letter!

b to say it is wrong to do something, or something is forbidden.
You mustn't tell lies.
Students mustn't smoke in the classrooms.

5 (not) have/had to are used:

a to talk about an obligation.
Robert has to be at work early tomorrow morning.
We had to write two compositions in class last week.

b to talk about a lack of obligation.
We don't have to go to school tomorrow. It's Sunday.
I didn't have to hand in any homework yesterday. The teacher didn't give us any.

6 may/might (not) are used:

a to talk about a possibility.
It may/might be a fine day tomorrow.

b to ask for or give permission formally.
May/Might I ask a question?

c May can be used to give permission formally.
You may leave the room for a few minutes.

7 should/ought to (do/have done) are used:

a to say that it is right or wrong to do something.
You should/ought to let your parents know where you are.
We shouldn't/ought not to have spent so much money yesterday.

b to say that something will almost certainly happen/ has almost certainly happened.
We should/ought to arrive home about 10 o'clock if the traffic isn't too heavy.
The plane should/ought to have taken off by now.

8 didn't need to (do)/needn't have (done) are used:

a to talk about what it was not necessary to do (and you didn't do it).
We didn't need to get up early so we stayed in bed until 11 o'clock.

b to talk about something that it was not necessary to do, but which you did.
We needn't have arrived at the airport so early because the plane was delayed.

UNIT 01 NEGATIVE PREFIXES p14

We can use prefixes like *un-*, *im-*, *in-* and *dis-* to make the meaning of words negative. We use:

im- before the letters *b*, *m* and *p*, e.g. *imbalance, immature, impossible.*

il- before the letter *l*, e.g. *illegal.*

i- before the letter *r*, e.g. *irresponsible.*

Un- and in- are very common negative prefixes, e.g. *unnecessary, unhappy, indecisive, incapable.*

UNIT 02 PRESENT TENSES p21

1 The present simple is used:

a to talk about things which happen regularly or are always true.
The sun sets in the west.

b with adverbs of time.
always, generally, usually, sometimes, hardly ever, never

c to talk about an event on a timetable.
The school terms starts on the 8th of January.

2 The present continuous is used:

a to talk about things that are happening at the moment.
The children are playing in the garden.

b to talk about things that are happening over a longer period of time.
Everything is becoming more expensive.

c with *always* to talk about something that happens on a regular basis and is annoying.
My brother is always borrowing my trainers.

3 Verbs rarely used in the present continuous:

Verbs which refer to states or conditions, not actions, are rarely used in the continuous form. Here are some examples:

Verbs of feeling
like, dislike, love, hate, need, want, prefer

Verbs of appearance
appear, seem

Verbs of possession
own, belong to, have

Verbs of physical perception
hear, smell, see, taste

Verbs of thinking
know, realise, suppose, understand, believe

UNIT 02 THE PASSIVE p21

The passive is used:

a when we are more interested in the subject of the sentence than in who did the action.
The ship was built in Norway.

b when we do not know who did the action.
My car was stolen last week.

c when the action and the person who did the action are both important.
An announcement was made by the ship's captain.

d in newspaper reports.
Two passengers were injured in a coach accident last night.

e to describe scientific experiments or processes.
The mixture was heated slowly.

f to describe what people in general think.
It is known that physical exercise is good for your health.

g when it is obvious or unimportant who does the action.
Our instructors are given the best training possible.

USING ADVERBS p21

1 **Adverbs are used to describe most verbs and are also used to describe adjectives, participles and other adverbs.**

adverb + verb	*Tania sings well.*
adverb + adjective	*The park is relatively big.*
adverb + participle	*These boats are very well made.*
adverb + adverb	*We found our way fairly easily.*

2 See Unit 8 for adverb position.

3 **Some adverbs of frequency (*sometimes, occasionally, generally*, etc.) can be used at the beginning of a sentence for emphasis.**
Sometimes, I enjoy sports.

4 **Forming adverbs**

a Most adverbs are formed by adding -ly to the adjective.
free, freely

b Some adverbs have the same form as the adjective.
hard, fast, early, late, far

c Some adverbs are very different from the adjectival form.
good – well

d Some adjectives ending in -ly do not have a corresponding adverb. If we want to use them as adverbs, we have to rephrase the sentence.
e.g. *friendly, lonely, silly, elderly*
She smiled at me in a friendly way.

UNIT 02 INFINITIVE FORMS p25

The infinitive can be used in different forms.
to teach
to be taught (passive)
to be teaching (continuous)
to have taught (perfect)
to have been taught (perfect passive)
to have been teaching (perfect continuous)

UNIT 03 COMPOUND ADJECTIVES p26

Compound adjectives are formed from two hyphenated words. Their meaning is usually clear.
left-handed, well-done, part-time, middle-aged, jaw-dropping, fun-filled

UNIT 03 *DESPITE, IN SPITE OF, ALTHOUGH* p29

The meaning of these words is similar, but they are used differently.

a We use *despite/in spite of* + a noun or the -*ing* form of the verb.
Despite/In spite of the heat, we went for a walk.
Despite/In spite of having no money, we had an enjoyable weekend.

b We use *although* + part of a sentence.
Although it was late, we decided to go out for a meal.
We went climbing although I didn't really want to go.

GRAMMAR REFERENCE

UNIT 03 PAST TENSES p31

1 The past simple is used:

a to talk about completed actions in the past.
I spent several months in Italy in 2002.

b with expressions that refer to points of time.
yesterday morning, last month, at midnight, on Sunday, in June, two weeks ago, the day before yesterday, when I was a teenager

c to describe a number of actions happening one after the other.
I got up early, had breakfast and caught the train.

2 The past continuous is used:

a to talk about things that were happening when another action took place.
I was driving to work when I heard the news.

b to set the scene in a story.
We were canoeing down the river, and the sun was shining.

3 used to + infinitive is used:

a to describe past habits.
I used to go to the cinema twice a week.

b to talk about an action which didn't happen in the past, but does now.
I didn't use to like going to the theatre.

c to describe past states or conditions.
The days used to seem longer when I was a child.

> **!** Would can also be used instead of *used to*, but it cannot be used to describe a state or condition, only an action.
> *My aunt would/used to feed the chickens every morning.*
> *She used to be a quiet sort of person.*

4 To be used to + -ing is used to talk about an action which (you) were accustomed to doing.
The children were used to travelling long distances by car.

5 To get used to + -ing is used to talk about an action which you became accustomed to doing.
It was hard work, but we soon got used to cycling in the mountains.

UNIT 03 ADJECTIVES ENDING IN -ED AND -ING p34

1 Adjectives ending in -ed are used to describe feelings.
I was bored by the film.
We weren't interested in listening to his excuses.

2 Adjectives ending in -ing are used to describe the quality of something or somebody.
The story was interesting.
He was a very boring speaker.

UNIT 04 MAKING SUGGESTIONS AND RECOMMENDATIONS p39

The verbs *suggest* and *recommend* are used:

a with *that*.
I suggest/recommend that you go to university.
They suggested/recommended that I went to university.

b with the -ing form of the verb.
I suggest painting the room blue.
I recommend painting the room blue.

> **!** When *suggest* is followed by the -ing form of the verb, the speaker is including him/herself in the suggested activity.
> *Paul suggested going to the cinema.*

UNIT 04 EMPHASISING A POINT p39

What can be used to mean *the thing(s) that* to emphasise a point at the beginning of the sentence, or after a verb as the object of a sentence.

What annoyed me was the way he spoke to the teacher.
I don't understand what you are talking about.

UNIT 04 THE FUTURE p40

1 going to (do) is used:

a to talk about an intention.
I'm going to stay in tonight.

b to talk about a probability based on evidence we have now.
It's going to be a nice afternoon.

2 The present continuous is used to talk about a definite future arrangement.
I'm having a job interview on Thursday.

3 Will is used:

a to express a willingness or offer to do something.
I'll help you with your homework.

b to make a request.
Will you help me with the washing up?

c to make an immediate decision.
I'll phone for a taxi!

d to make a promise.
I won't let you down!

e to express determination.
I will pass my driving test!

f to make a prediction.
He'll come home soon.

g to express an inability or refusal to do something.
This key won't turn in the lock.
I won't forgive you for what you said!

4 Shall is used:

a to make a suggestion.
Shall we go for a pizza?

b to make an offer.
Shall I post those letters for you?

5 The present simple is used to talk about a future event, e.g. on a timetable.
The summer holidays begin on Friday.

6 The future continuous is used to talk about an action which will be taking place at a certain time in the future.
This time next week, we'll be travelling to Switzerland.

7 The future perfect is used to talk about an action which will be finished before a certain time in the future.
I'll have finished this homework by six o'clock.

UNIT 04 *BOUND TO, LIKELY TO* p44

a *Bound to* means *certain to happen*.
It's bound to rain tomorrow.
Ted's bound to miss the train. He always does.

b *Likely to* means *there is a good chance of this happening*.
It's likely to be a difficult journey.

! *Likely* can be used as an adjective with the same meaning as *likely to*, but *bound to* cannot be used in this way.
They say it's going to be a hot summer, but I don't think that's very likely, do you?

UNIT 04 *HAD BETTER (NOT)* p44

Had better (do) means *it would be better if (you) did*.
We had better order a taxi.
You'd better ring for an ambulance.

UNIT 04 OTHER WAYS OF TALKING ABOUT THE FUTURE p45

Be about to, be on the point of (be ready to) and *be due to (be expected to)* can also be used to talk about the future.
I was about to give Dave a call when the phone rang.
We were on the point of leaving when some unexpected guests arrived.
The plane is due to take off in ten minutes' time.

UNIT 05 COMPARING ADJECTIVES AND ADVERBS p49

a Most single-syllable adjectives and adverbs are compared using -er and -est.
old, older, the oldest (person)
(working) hard, harder, the hardest

b Two-syllable adjectives ending in -y, e.g. *friendly, wealthy, easy* and some others, e.g. *clever, quiet, narrow* also follow this pattern.
Last week's test was much easier.
My brother is cleverer than I am.

c Most other adjectives and adverbs with two or more syllables are compared with *more, the most*.
Tigers are dangerous animals.
Lions are more dangerous than tigers.
Hungry lions are the most dangerous animals of all.

d We can also compare equal things and make negative comparisons with adjectives and adverbs using *as … as* and *not as … as*.
He's as old as me – we're both 19.
I do not speak English as fluently as my sister.

e The most common irregular comparatives and superlatives are:
good/better/best (adjective)
well/better/best (adverb)
bad/worse/the worst (adjective)
badly/worse/the worst (adverb)

f The present perfect is often used with superlatives.
She is the nicest person I have ever met.

UNIT 05 THE PRESENT PERFECT p51

1 The present perfect simple is used:

a to talk about a non-specific time in the past, i.e. when no time is mentioned.
I've bought a new bicycle.

b to talk about a present situation which is the result of a previous action.
You've torn your jacket.

c with adverbs of time, e.g. *already (before now), just (recently), still* and *yet, ever* and *never*.
already/just
Have you (already) seen this film (already)?
Yes, we've just finished watching it.
still (to talk about an on-going situation)
The programme still hasn't finished.
Has the programme still not finished?
yet (This hasn't happened but is expected to.)
Has the film finished yet?
I haven't done my homework yet.
ever (at any time up to the present)
Have you ever been to Spain?
never (at no time in the past)
I've never been to a disco.

d with prepositions or prepositional phrases, e.g. *this morning, so far, up to now*, to talk about actions which are still going on or which have just finished.
We've studied two different books this term.
I've worked hard over the last two days.

e with *been* and *gone* to convey a different meaning.
Ben has been to Madrid. (He is not there now.)
Ben has gone to Madrid. (He is there now.)

f with *for* and *since* to talk about how long something has lasted and when it began.
Ben has worked here for two months.
Ben has been here since the end of last month.

g with ordinals or a superlative.
This is the third time I've been to this nightclub.
That was the best film I have ever seen.

2 The present perfect continuous is used:

a to emphasise the length of an action, which may still be going on.
The band have been rehearsing for hours!
I've been revising since 8.30 this morning.

b to express anger or irritation at the length of time an action has taken.
I've been trying to phone you all morning!

UNIT 06 CAUSATIVES p61

The causative *have* or *get something (done)* is used when somebody else does something for you. It is quite often used when describing a service which you pay for.
We had our house painted last week.
I got my hair cut yesterday.
Bill's going to get the car serviced tomorrow.

UNIT 06 THE PAST PERFECT p61

1 The past perfect simple is used:

a in a sentence usually containing another verb in the past simple, for an action which happened before another in the past.
The passengers had waited for almost two hours before the train arrived.

b to report a verb in the present perfect or past simple in indirect speech.
'I've never been on a cruise before,' said my aunt.
My aunt said that she had never been on a cruise before.
'I visited a friend in hospital once,' said my aunt.
My aunt said she had visited a friend in hospital once.

2 The past perfect continuous is used:

a in a sentence usually containing another verb in the past simple, for an action which had been happening before another in the past.
The rescue team had been digging for several hours when they suddenly heard the sound of voices.

b to report a verb in the present perfect continuous or past continuous in indirect speech.
'I've been taking the dog for a walk,' said my uncle.
My uncle said that he had been taking the dog for a walk.
'I was watching TV when I heard the news,' said Polly.
Polly said she had been watching TV when she heard the news.

UNIT 06 + THE -ING FORM OF THE VERB p63

1 The -ing form of the verb is used:

a after an adjective followed by a preposition.
I'm not very fond of reading.
I get fed up with listening to the radio.

b as the object of a verb.
I like swimming.
I can't stand playing football.

2 See Units 7 and 9 for verbs that can be followed by -ing or the infinitive.

UNIT 07 VERBS FOLLOWED BY -ING OR THE INFINITIVE p69

1 Verbs + -ing form

a A number of common verbs and expressions are usually followed by the -ing form rather than the infinitive.
I enjoy travelling.
Other common verbs that follow this pattern are:
appreciate, avoid, can't help, can't stand, consider, deny, dislike, enjoy, feel like, finish, give up, it's not worth, it's no use, keep on, look forward to, mention, mind, miss, object to, practise, put off, risk, suggest, there's no point

! Remember that all verbs usually take the -ing form after a preposition.

b Some verbs are followed by an object + preposition + -ing form.
May I congratulate you on winning this award.
Other common verbs that follow this pattern are:
apologize to sb for, accuse sb of, blame sb for, prevent sb from, protect sb from, thank sb for

2 Verbs + infinitive

a Some verbs are followed by the infinitive rather than the -ing form.
I want to stay in and watch a film on TV tonight.
Other common verbs that follow this pattern are:
afford, appear, arrange, decide, expect, fail, happen, hope, intend, learn, manage, offer, plan, prepare, pretend, promise, refuse, seem, threaten, want

b *Make* and *let* are followed by an infinitive without *to*.
They made me play games every afternoon.

c Some verbs are followed by an object + infinitive.
Ted has asked me to go to the cinema on Saturday night.
Other common verbs that follow this pattern are:
advise, allow, enable, encourage, force, invite, order, persuade, remind, teach, tell

UNIT 07 REPORTED SPEECH p71

1 Leaving the tense unchanged

There is no need to make any tense changes if the reporting verb is in the present tense and the statement is still true.

'I love sports clothes.' (my sister)
My sister says she loves sports clothes.

2 Making tense changes

If the reporting verb is in the past tense, we usually have to change the tenses.

Actual words	Reported speech
Imperative	Infinitive
'Don't forget!'	*She told him not to forget.*
Present simple	Past simple
'I am late.'	*He said he was late.*
Present continuous	Past continuous
'She's wearing jeans.'	*They said she was wearing jeans.*
Past simple	Past perfect
'The manager phoned.'	*He said that the manager had phoned.*
Past continuous	Past perfect continuous
'We were shopping for shoes.'	*They said that they had been shopping for shoes.*
Present perfect simple	Past perfect simple
'No one has phoned.'	*She said that no one had phoned.*
Present perfect continuous	Past perfect continuous
'Tim's been working too hard.'	*She said Tim had been working too hard.*
Past perfect	Past perfect (no change)
'I had never been there before.'	*He said that he had never been there before.*

3 Other changes to make

If dates, times and places have been mentioned, make the following changes.

today	that day
yesterday	the day before, the previous day
tomorrow	the next day, the following day, the day after
here	there
this (restaurant)	that (restaurant)

UNIT 07 REPORTING QUESTIONS p71

a The tense changes in reported questions are exactly the same as in reported statements.

b When reporting direct questions, we use the word *if* or *whether* before the question.
'Did you arrive late?'
She asked me if I had arrived late.

c When reporting a question which begins with a question word, e.g. *who, which, where, why, when, how,* we repeat the question word.
'Where did you buy the tracksuit?'
He asked me where I had bought the tracksuit.

d The word order in reported questions is reversed to subject + verb (not verb + subject).
'Are you hungry?' (Robin)
Robin wondered if we were hungry.

e Double questions also reverse order in this way.
'Could you tell me where the stadium is?'
Robin asked us if we could tell him where the stadium was.

! Question marks are not used in reported questions.

UNIT 08 THE ORDER OF ADJECTIVES p78–79

When two or more adjectives appear before a noun, we put them in this order:

your opinion	>	lovely
size/weight	>	long
age	>	old
shape	>	square
colour	>	red
country of origin	>	Chinese
material	>	silk
noun	>	scarf

! Do not try to use too many adjectives before a noun. Two or three are usually enough.

UNIT 08 THE POSITION OF ADVERBS p79

Adverbs can be placed:

a between the auxiliary verb and the main verb.
I have always liked pizza.

b between the subject of a sentence and a regular verb.
I never go to the theatre.

c after a verb like *to be*, or a modal.
You're incredibly talented.
You must never tell anyone what I've just told you.

UNIT 08 CONDITIONALS p80

a The zero conditional (*if* + present tense, + present tense) is used when *if* means *whenever* or *every time*.
If people drink too quickly, they often get hiccups.

b The first conditional (*if* + present simple or continuous, or present perfect, + *will* or a modal + infinitive) is used to talk about things which might happen in the future.
If you go out in this rain, you'll get soaked.
If you phone Jim now, you may be able to get hold of him.
If you're not doing anything, could you help me prepare the vegetables?
If you've finished doing your homework, we can go for a swim.
If you want to get a good mark in the exam, you must study harder.

GRAMMAR REFERENCE

c The second conditional (*if* + past simple or continuous, + *would* or a modal + infinitive) is used to talk about imaginary or unlikely situations, and to give advice.
If I were a film star, I would be very rich.
If I were you, I'd take a break from studying.
If I was studying languages at college, I could live abroad for a year.

d The third conditional (*if* + past perfect simple or continuous, + *would have* or a modal + the past participle of the verb), is used to speculate about what happened in the past.
If I had been at home, I would have answered your call.
If we hadn't won the lottery, we couldn't have gone on holiday.
If I hadn't been watching TV, I might have heard the doorbell ring.

UNIT 08 *UNLESS* AND *IN CASE* p80

a *Unless* means *if not*.
James wouldn't phone at this time of night unless it was important.

b *In case* is quite different from *if*.

If is used to explain that you do one thing if another event happens.
If I have time, I'll go to the library.

In case is used to explain that you do something anyway even if the other event might not happen.
I'll take my mobile phone, in case I need to contact you urgently.

UNIT 08 REFLEXIVE PRONOUNS p84

1 **The pronouns *myself, yourself, him/herself, ourselves, yourselves* and *themselves* are used when the object of the verb refers back to the subject.**
I taught myself to paint.
Come on, help yourselves.
They cannot be separated from the verb they belong to.

2 **See Unit 10 for emphasising pronouns.**

UNIT 09 *REGRET DOING/REGRET TO DO* p91

a We use the -*ing* form after some verbs, e.g. *regret doing/ remember doing*, when we are sorry about, or haven't forgotten what we did.
I regret telling Angela about the party.
I remember visiting this place when I was a child.

b We use the infinitive with *to* after some verbs, e.g. *regret to tell/remember to tell*, when we are sorry about or need to remember what we are about to do.
I regret to say that I can't offer you the job.
Please remember to post my letter.

UNIT 09 WISHES AND REGRETS p91

I wish/If only are used:

a to express regret about a present situation. We use *I wish/If only* + the past form of the verb.
I wish I could come with you on holiday.
If only I was/were better at languages.

b to express regret about a past action. We use *I wish/ If only* + the past perfect.
I wish I hadn't bought those shoes.
If only I had listened to my mother.

c to complain about someone's behaviour. We use *I wish/If only* + *would (not)* + infinitive.
I wish Michael wouldn't leave his dirty clothes on the floor.
I wish you wouldn't make that noise.

! We never say *I wish I would*, we say *I wish I could.*

UNIT 09 REFLEXIVE PRONOUNS AS EMPHASISERS p94

We can use reflexive pronouns emphatically to stress that someone did something on their own, without help. They follow the object of the verb.
I wrote this essay myself.
They are often used with *by*.
Sam decorated this room all by himself.

UNIT 09 OTHER VERBS THAT CAN BE FOLLOWED BY -*ING* OR THE INFINITIVE p95

a Some verbs can be followed by either the -*ing* form or infinitive, and there is no difference in meaning.
We started to revise/revising for our exams last month.
Other verbs like this are:
begin, intend, continue

b Verbs of perception (*see, hear, watch*, etc.) are usually followed by the -*ing* form if we see part of the action, and by the infinitive if we see all of the action.
I saw the horses running across the field.
(I noticed that they were there.)
I saw the current tennis champion play against a tough opponent yesterday.
(I saw the whole tennis match.)

c Some verbs change in meaning when followed by the -*ing* form or infinitive.
I like going for a swim. (I enjoy doing it.)
I like to go for a swim once a week. (I choose to do it.)

UNIT 10 *BEFORE, AFTER, WHEN, WHILE +*
-ING p99

Instead of using a subordinate clause, e.g. *Before I finished,*
While I was studying, we can use *before, after, when,*
while + -ing.

While spending a holiday in the Mediterranean, we met an
old friend.

Even though you don't mention the subject of the *-ing*
form of the verb, the subject of the other part of the
sentence must be the same.

While cycling home, Bob had a flat tyre.

UNIT 10 RELATIVE CLAUSES p101

1 Defining relative clauses

Defining relative clauses make it clear which person
or thing we are talking about.

a We can use relative pronouns such as *who, which,*
where or *that* to refer to people or things.
The director who/that made this film is very well known.
This is the place where Shakespeare was born.

b The relative pronoun can be left out if it is the
object of a verb.
This is the restaurant (–) I was talking about yesterday.

c The relative pronoun *whose* refers to possession.
I met an artist whose work is famous.

d *Whom* can be used as an object pronoun referring to
a person, but *who* or *that* are also acceptable.
The film director who(m)/that I talked to was very
interesting.

e If the relative pronoun comes after a preposition
such as *to, from, with*, etc. *whom* must be used.
The student who I was talking to was very intelligent.
The student to whom I was talking was very intelligent.

2 Non-defining relative clauses

Non-defining relative clauses contain additional
information about a person or thing already
mentioned.

a Commas are always used around the non-defining
relative clause.

b The pronoun cannot be left out and it is not
possible to use *that.*

c You can use *which* to refer to things, *who* to refer to
people, *when* to refer to time and *where* to refer to
places.
My notebook, which was here a minute ago, seems to
have disappeared.
The winter, when the weather is severe, is not a good
time to visit Alaska.
I often go back to that beach, where my parents have a
caravan.

WRITING GUIDE

INFORMAL TRANSACTIONAL EMAIL

1 Read the exam task and the sample answer.

You have received an email from your English-speaking friend Mark, who wants to come and do a language course in your country. Read the email and the notes you have made. Then write an email to Mark, using all your notes.

Write 120–150 words.

From: Mark Davies
Sent: 18th April
Subject: Language course

Hi there Jan!

I wonder if you could you do something for me. I want to come and do a language course in your country and I need some information. *(When and how long for?)*

Are there any schools near you that just do courses either in the morning or the afternoon? Could you also give me some idea of how much a course like this would cost? *(Yes, recommend one)* *(Give details)*

And just one more thing – would it be possible to stay with you while I'm doing the course? *(Unfortunately, no because ...)*

Hope to hear from you soon.

Mark

SAMPLE ANSWER

From: Jan Verhoeven
Sent: 20th April
Subject: Language course

Hi Mark. How are you?

Thanks for your received email that you have sent. I'm much glad to have it. I am happy that you will coming to do a language course in my country. I try to give you some information. I am not sure but I think that there are some language schools near me that do courses, but they costs a lot of money. I going to find out and send you broshure. I think it is useful. I am sorry but you can't to stay with me – that is because we have no rooms at the moment. We try find you place to stay. Maybe with a host family.

Your friend

Jan

2 Using the checklist, decide what kind of mark this answer might get: good, adequate or inadequate. Then read the examiner's comments.

	Yes	No
The correct format (email)?	☐	☐
Grammar and spelling accurate?	☐	☐
Suitable register (informal)?	☐	☐
All the points covered?	☐	☐
The right length?	☐	☐
Well organised with paragraphs and link words?	☐	☐
A good range of language, e.g. asking for and giving information, making a suggestion?	☐	☐

» EXAMINER'S COMMENTS

Although the reply is in the correct form and register, there are many grammar mistakes: 'your received email', 'I'm much glad', 'I am happy that you will coming', 'I try to give you', 'they costs a lot of money', 'I going to find out and send you broshure', 'you can't to stay with me', 'We try find you place to stay'. There is only one spelling mistake: 'broshure'. The first points are not covered. There are some link words but no paragraphs. The main text of the email is only 113 words. This answer would get an inadequate mark.

FORMAL TRANSACTIONAL LETTER

1 Read the exam task and the sample answer.

Your school is organising an exchange trip to the USA. Read the letter sent out to students and the notes you have made. Then write a letter to the school director, using all your notes. Write 120–150 words.

Dear students

I am writing to inform you about an interesting event which will take place <u>next summer</u>. The school is organising an exchange trip with a school in the USA. Accommodation will be provided by American students taking part in the exchange, and you in turn will be expected to <u>provide the same for them</u>. <u>All you will need to pay for</u> will be your flights to and from the USA.

If you <u>would like to take part in the exchange</u>, all you have to do is complete the enclosed form and hand it in to the school secretary. If you have any questions, please do not hesitate to contact me.

Yours sincerely

P Kelly

Patricia Kelly, School Director

When? / How long exactly?

All meals included?

How much spending money needed?

Absolutely!

SAMPLE ANSWER

Dear Mrs Kelly

Thank you for your letter about the exchange trip to the USA. It seems very interesting and I would very much like to take part in the exchange. However, I would like to know a little bit more about it before I make my desicion.

First, can you tell me exactly when the exchange will take place next summer and how long it will last? You mention accommodation, but does this include providing meals as well? And finally, could you give me some idea of how much spending money we might need to take with us?

I am looking forward to receive your reply. When I know a few more details about the trip, I will complete the form and hand it in to the school secretary.

Yours sincerely

David Martin

2 Using the checklist, decide what kind of mark this answer might get: good, adequate or inadequate. Then read the examiner's comment.

	Yes	No
The correct format (letter)?	☐	☐
Grammar and spelling accurate?	☐	☐
Suitable register (formal)?	☐	☐
All the points covered?	☐	☐
The right length?	☐	☐
Well organised with paragraphs and link words?	☐	☐
A good range of language, e.g. asking for and giving information, expressing interest?	☐	☐

›› EXAMINER'S COMMENTS

The reply is well organised and the right length (127 words for the main text). There is only one spelling mistake, 'desicion' instead of 'decision', and one grammar mistake, 'receive' instead of 'receiving'. All the points are covered and the register and language are suitable. The answer would get a good mark.

ARTICLE

1 Read the exam task and the sample answer.

You have seen this announcement on the school notice board.

> ### MY FAVOURITE TV PROGRAMME
>
> Tell us about your favourite TV programme. We will publish the most interesting articles in our next issue of the school magazine.

Write your article in 120–180 words in an appropriate style.

SAMPLE ANSWER

My favourite TV programme

My favourite TV programme's a talent contest where unknown people show viewers what they can do. After there performances, the judges decide who should win the contest.

Although some of the people on the show are'nt really very good, there are usually one or two who are very good indeed. While some of them may not be as good as professionals entertainers, it is very intresting to watch them and try to guess who might win.

The programme is excited and a lot of people watch it. This is probably because it is quite funny to see how the people behave when they win and lose.

I like the programme because it gives ordinary people a chance to be famous.

2 Using the checklist, decide what kind of mark this answer might get: good, adequate or inadequate. Then read the examiner's comments.

	Yes	No
The correct format (article)?	☐	☐
Grammar and spelling accurate?	☐	☐
Suitable register (neutral)?	☐	☐
The right length?	☐	☐
Well organised with paragraphs and link words?	☐	☐
A good range of structures and vocabulary?	☐	☐
Target reader fully informed	☐	☐

›› EXAMINER'S COMMENTS

The article is just within the lower word limit (120 words). There are two contractions, which are not appropriate in style, but there are only two spelling mistakes: 'intresting' instead of 'interesting', and 'there performances' instead of 'their performances'. There are two incorrect uses of adjectives: 'professionals entertainers' and 'excited'. Despite the rather narrow range of structures and vocabulary, the reader would be informed and the answer would get an adequate mark.

REPORT

1 Read the exam task and the sample answer.

Your school has been given quite a large sum of money to spend on a new facility for students. The Principal has asked you to write a report suggesting what kinds of things the school might spend the money on.

Write your report in 120–180 words.

SAMPLE ANSWER

A new facility for students

There are several things the school could provide for students.

Computer room

Although the school has some computers which students can use, there are not enough for the large number of students. Many students do not have the internet at home so what they need is be able to use the internet whenever they want to at school. A new computer room would make this possible for students.

Fitness centre

Some students travel a long way to school, and they have no time when they get home to take any physical exercise. If the school had a fitness centre, students could use this in their lunch break or their free periods. This would be very popular with students.

Café

At the moment, students bring a packed lunch to school or buy something in the shops outside the school. A café which is provided healthy but cheap food would be a place where students could meet their friends and relax.

I would definitely recommend choosing one of the suggestions above.

2 Using the checklist, decide what kind of mark this answer might get: good, adequate or inadequate. Then read the examiner's comments.

	Yes	No
The correct format (report)?	☐	☐
Includes some factual information?	☐	☐
Some suggestions and/or recommendations?	☐	☐
Grammar and spelling accurate?	☐	☐
Suitable style (neutral)?	☐	☐
The right length?	☐	☐
A good range of structures and vocabulary?	☐	☐

›› EXAMINER'S COMMENTS

The report is the right length (169 words, including the headings within the report). It includes relevant information and is clearly organised. There is a good range of language and structures and there are very few mistakes: 'is be able' instead of 'is to be able', and 'a café which is provided' instead of 'a café which provided'. The style is suitably neutral. This answer would get a good mark.

WRITING GUIDE

ESSAY

1 **Read the exam task and the sample answer.**

Your class has had a discussion on what it must be like to be famous. As a follow-up, your teacher has asked you to write an essay answering the following question and giving reasons for your opinions.

Why would anyone want to be famous?

Write your essay in 120–180 words.

SAMPLE ANSWER

Why would anyone want to be famous?

I can't think there is anyone in the world who does not want to be a famous person. I'm sure that everyone would like to be famous for some reason. Everybody would like to earn a lot of money and to be someone everybody else knows and wants to meet.

People who are famous can do anything they want to do. They can go anywhere. They can buy anything. They can live in the house they want to. They can buy the clothes they want to. They can have lots of friends and go to the best restaurants. You get a good table in a restaurant and you can choose the very expensive things when you buy something. If you go out for walking in the street, everybody wants to talk to you. Everyone wants to shake your hands. So I think it's grate to be famous. You know you are a very special person and everybody thinks you are a very special person.

2 Using the checklist, decide what kind of mark this answer might get: good, adequate or inadequate. Then read the examiner's comments.

	Yes	No
Presents both points of view?	☐	☐
Includes some opinions?	☐	☐
Grammar and spelling accurate?	☐	☐
Suitable style (neutral)?	☐	☐
The right length?	☐	☐
Well organised with paragraphs and link words?	☐	☐
A good range of structures and vocabulary?	☐	☐

» EXAMINER'S COMMENTS

Although the essay is the right length (164 words), it does not attempt to present more than one point of view, which would give the writer more opportunities to show a range of language and structures. There is only one spelling mistake: 'grate' instead of 'great'. The grammar is mostly correct with few mistakes: 'you can choose the very expensive things' instead of 'choose very expensive things' or 'choose the most expensive things', and 'If you go out for walking' instead of 'for a walk'. However, there is a lot of repetition in the essay, there are only two rather disjointed paragraphs, and the style changes awkwardly from using 'they' (to talk about people in general) to 'you'. Therefore this answer would get only an adequate mark.

LETTER BASED ON A SET BOOK

1 Read the exam task and the sample answer.

Ghost stories – Oxford Bookworms Collection
The Ghost Coach by Amelia B. Edwards

This is part of a letter from an English friend of yours.

> I saw a film on television called The Ghost Coach. I think you told me you had read the story. What did you think of it?

Write a letter to your friend, giving your opinion. Do not write any postal addresses. Write your answer in 120–180 words.

SAMPLE ANSWER

Dear Peter

Thanks for your letter. You asked me about the ghost story I read. I thought it was very well-written. From the begining, I felt that I knew the main character, and what happened to him was very real. He tells his story as if he is actually speaking to you.

The fact that the story is set in a lonley place and the writer gets lost in the snow creates a good atmosphere. The characters he meets also seem very strange.

I thought the bit about the coach and the people who had been killed in an accident a long time ago was very frightening. And when the writer began to realise that the coach he was going to take was the one in the accident, I felt really terrified.

What I did liked about the story was that it was never been explained how the writer had been a passenger on the ghost coach. But I was glad the story had a happy ending. I hope you enjoyed the film as much as I liked the story.

All the best

Maria

2 Using the checklist, decide what kind of mark this answer might get: good, adequate or inadequate. Then read the examiner's comments.

	Yes	No
The correct format (a letter)?	☐	☐
Opinions expressed, with reasons?	☐	☐
Refers in detail to the story read?	☐	☐
Grammar and spelling accurate?	☐	☐
Suitable style (informal)?	☐	☐
The right length?	☐	☐
Well organised with paragraphs and link words?	☐	☐
A good range of structures and vocabulary?	☐	☐

» EXAMINER'S COMMENTS

The answer is in the correct format and is well-organised. The writer has given reasons for her opinions and related them to the story that she has read. The main text of the letter is at the top end of the word limit (179 words). There are some grammar and spelling mistakes: 'what I did liked' instead of 'did like', 'it was never been explained' instead of 'it was never explained', only one 'n' in the middle of 'beginning' and 'lonley' for 'lonely'. However, the letter is written in a suitable style (informal) and there is a range of structures. The answer would get a good mark.

REVIEW

1 Read the exam task and the sample answer.

You have been asked to write a review in English for your school magazine. The review must have this heading:

> ### THE BEST FILM I HAVE EVER SEEN

Write your review in 120–180 words.

SAMPLE ANSWER

For my birthday I recieved a film on DVD called *The Visitors*. The film was in French, but it had English subtitles.

It was the funniest film I have ever seen, and the story was unusual and interesting. Two people from the Middle Ages, a rich knight and his servant, drank a liquid and found that they were transported into modern times.

Everything they saw and did was new for them, and they kept making silly mistakes. You never knew what they were going to do next. Looking at our modern life through the eyes of these two people was really entertaining.

In the end, the servant stayed in the modern time and became the owner of the castle where the knight had lived hundreds of years ago. The knight went back to the Middle Ages and married his fiancée.

I recommend you to see the film. The acting is very good and you will really enjoy the story.

2 Using the checklist, decide what kind of mark this answer might get: good, adequate or inadequate. Then read the examiner's comments.

	Yes	No
Includes descriptions of the characters and story?	☐	☐
Target reader fully informed?	☐	☐
Grammar and spelling accurate?	☐	☐
Suitable style (neutral)?	☐	☐
The right length?	☐	☐
Clearly organised with paragraphs and link words?	☐	☐
A good range of structures and vocabulary?	☐	☐

›› EXAMINER'S COMMENTS

The review includes descriptions about the characters and story. There are very few mistakes: 'recieved' instead of 'received', 'in the modern time' instead of 'in modern times' and 'I recommend you to see' instead of 'recommend that you see' or 'recommend seeing'. The style is suitable and the ideas are clearly organised. There is a range of structures and vocabulary, the text is a good length (159 words), and the target reader would be fully informed. The answer would get a good mark.

STORY

1 **Read the exam task and the sample answer.**

You recently saw this advertisement in a magazine.

> Enter our short story competition. The story
> must begin with the following words.
> *As Jim was walking to school one morning,
> something quite unexpected happened.*
> The best entries will be published in the next
> issue of our magazine.

Write your story in 120–180 words.

SAMPLE ANSWER

As Jim was walking to school one morning, something quite unexpected happened. He saw his good friend. It was long time that he didn't see his friend. His friend moved another town. He was pleased that he has seen his friend and they said a lot of things. His friend studied the same things he studied at school. His friend wanted to go in university – like him.

After a long time, Jim said goodbye his friend. He promised he will email his friend and his friend promised to email him, too. Later, his friend sends an email to him. Jim was very surprised and happy when he meet his friend and he thought his friend was happy to see him, too. He did not expect to meet him when he was walking to school one morning so it was very unexpected.

2 **Using the checklist, decide what kind of mark this answer might get: good, adequate or inadequate. Then read the examiner's comments.**

	Yes	No
Follows on from the prompt sentence?	☐	☐
Holds the reader's interest?	☐	☐
Interesting or unexpected ending?	☐	☐
Grammar and spelling accurate?	☐	☐
Correct style (neutral or informal)?	☐	☐
The right length?	☐	☐
Well organised with paragraphs and link words?	☐	☐
A good range of structures and vocabulary?	☐	☐

» EXAMINER'S COMMENTS

The story is the right length (141 words), and it follows on from the prompt sentence. However, there is nothing particularly interesting or unexpected about either the story or the ending, and nothing very much happens as a result of the chance meeting. The grammar and spelling are inaccurate in places: 'was long time that he didn't see his friend', 'His friend moved another town', 'He was pleased that he has seen his friend', ' the same things he studied at school', 'he promised he will email his friend', and 'happy when he meet his friend'. There are also some missing prepositions, or the wrong preposition is used. The style is consistent and there are a few link words, but there is a lot of repetition and a narrow range of vocabulary or inappropriate vocabulary, and there are no adverbs. The answer would get an inadequate mark.

EXAM OVERVIEW

INTRODUCTION

The First Certificate of English corresponds to Level Three in the Cambridge ESOL five-level system. It also corresponds to the Association of Language Teachers in Europe (ALTE) Level Three, and Council of Europe level B2.

There are five papers in the examination, each worth 20% of the total marks. To achieve a passing grade (A, B or C) candidates must achieve approximately 60% of the total marks available, or above. Candidates' grades are based on the total score from all five papers and there is no pass or fail grade for individual papers.

PAPER 1 READING (1 HOUR)

This paper has three parts, each with a text or texts and comprehension questions. There are 30 questions in total.

The texts may consist of several short pieces, and the length of each text may be between 550–700 words.

The texts are taken from newspapers, magazines, reports, fiction, advertisements, leaflets, brochures, etc.

Part	Task type	Number of items	What you do	What it tests	How to do it
1	Multiple choice	8	Choose the best answer from four option multiple-choice questions.	Your understanding of a text and opinions expressed in it.	pages 6, 36, 66, 96
2	Missing sentences	7	Decide where sentences belong in a text.	Your understanding of text structure and development.	pages 16, 46, 76
3	Multiple matching	15	Match prompts from a list to elements in a text.	Your ability to find specific information.	pages 26, 56, 86

MARKS

One mark for each correct answer to the multiple-matching tasks.

Two marks for each correct answer to the multiple-choice and missing sentences tasks.

PAPER 2 WRITING (1 HOUR 20 MINUTES)

This paper has two parts. The Part 1 question is a compulsory letter or email, and is based on input information. In Part 2 you choose one question from four; Question 5 has two options on a set reading text.

Answers for Part 1 should be 120–150 words in length, and for Part 2 120–180 words.

The task types for Part 2 will be from the following: article, essay, letter, report, review, story.

Examples of Paper 2 question types can be found in the Writing Guide on pages 116–123.

Part	Task type	Number of items	What you do	What it tests	How to do it
1	Compulsory contextualised task based on input material of up to 160 words, which could be from advertisements, extracts from letters, emails, etc.	One compulsory task.	Write according to the task instructions.	Your ability to process input material and select and apply it according to the instructions.	pages 8, 18, 88, 98
2	Contextualised task in no more than 70 words.	One from a choice of four questions; Question 5 has two options.		Your ability to write according to the instructions, in the correct style, layout and register in order to have a positive effect on the reader.	pages 28, 38, 48, 58, 68, 78

MARKS

Parts 1 and 2 have equal marks.

PAPER 3 USE OF ENGLISH (45 MINUTES)

This paper has four parts, and a total of 42 questions.

The testing focus is on understanding and controlling formal elements of language (e.g. grammar, word formation, spelling).

Part	Task type	Number of items	What you do	What it tests	How to do it
1	Multiple-choice cloze	12	Fill 12 gaps in a text choosing from four-option multiple-choice items.	Phrases, collocations, idioms, phrasal verbs, linkers, used to complete a text with the correct meaning and grammatical context.	pages 10, 50, 90
2	Open cloze	12	Fill 12 gaps in a text with one word per gap.	Your awareness and control of structural items.	pages 20, 60
3	Word formation	10	Form appropriate words from prompts to complete 10 gaps in a text.	Word formation.	pages 30, 70, 100
4	Key word transformations	8	Complete a gapped sentence with two to five words, including a key word, so that it has the same meaning as the lead-in sentence.	Your awareness and control of grammatical and lexical items.	pages 40, 80

MARKS

Parts 1, 2 and 3: one mark for each correct answer.

Part 4: each answer receives up to 2 marks.

PAPER 4 LISTENING (APPROX. 40 MINUTES)

This paper has four parts, and 30 questions.

The recorded texts may include the following:

Monologues: announcements, radio broadcasts, telephone messages, speeches, talks, lectures, etc.

Conversations between two or three speakers: conversations, interviews, discussions.

The testing focus is on understanding specific information, gist, attitude, opinion, main points and detail.

All parts are heard twice. The instructions are given on the question paper and are also heard. The recordings include a variety of voices, styles of delivery and accents.

Part	Task type	Number of items	What you do	What it tests	How to do it
1	Multiple choice	8	Listen to eight unrelated extracts and choose the best answer from three-option multiple-choice items.	Your understanding of gist, detail, function, purpose, attitude, situation, genre, etc.	pages 12, 52
2	Sentence completion	10	Listen to a monologue or text involving interacting speakers and complete gaps in sentences with information from the text.	Your understanding of detail, specific information, stated opinion.	pages 22, 62, 92
3	Multiple matching	5	Listen to five short related monologues and select the correct option from a list of six.	As Part 1.	pages 32, 72, 102
4	Multiple choice	7	Listen to a monologue or text involving interacting speakers and choose the best answer from three-option multiple-choice items.	Your understanding of opinion, attitude, gist, main idea, specific information.	pages 42, 82

MARKS

One mark for each correct answer.

Spelling must be correct for common words and those considered easy to spell.

PAPER 5 SPEAKING (APPROX. 14 MINUTES)

This paper has four parts.

The standard format is two candidates and two examiners, one acting as interlocutor and assessor, the other acting as assessor only. In certain circumstances, three candidates may sit the test together.

Part	Task type	Length	What you do	What it tests	How to do it
1	A conversation between the interlocutor and each candidate.	3 minutes	Ask and answer 'personal' questions.	Your ability to use general interactional and social language.	pages 13, 63
2	Individual long turns and brief responses.	1 minute long turn for each candidate and 20-second response from the second candidate.	Talk about visual prompts.	Your ability to describe, compare, express opinions.	pages 23, 43, 73, 93
3	Two-way interaction between candidates.	3 minutes	Discuss a problem-solving task based on visual and/or written prompts.	Your ability to exchange ideas, express and justify opinions, agree and disagree, speculate, reach a decision through negotiation, etc.	pages 33, 53, 83, 103
4	A discussion between candidates and the interlocutor.	4 minutes	Discuss issues related to the Part 3 topic.	Your ability to express and justify opinions, agree and/or disagree.	pages 33, 53, 83, 103

MARKS

Candidates are assessed on their performance throughout the test in the following areas:

- Grammar and vocabulary (accuracy and appropriacy)

- Discourse management (ability to express ideas in coherent, connected speech)

- Pronunciation (individual sounds, linking of words, stress and intonation)

- Interactive communication (turn-taking, initiating and responding)

- Global achievement (overall effectiveness in the tasks)

The assessor marks according to detailed Analytical Scales, the interlocutor gives a mark on a Global Scale, which is less detailed.

OXFORD
UNIVERSITY PRESS

Great Clarendon Street, Oxford OX2 6DP

Oxford University Press is a department of the University of Oxford.
It furthers the University's objective of excellence in research, scholarship,
and education by publishing worldwide in

Oxford New York

Auckland Cape Town Dar es Salaam Hong Kong Karachi
Kuala Lumpur Madrid Melbourne Mexico City Nairobi
New Delhi Shanghai Taipei Toronto

With offices in

Argentina Austria Brazil Chile Czech Republic France Greece
Guatemala Hungary Italy Japan Poland Portugal Singapore
South Korea Switzerland Thailand Turkey Ukraine Vietnam

OXFORD and OXFORD ENGLISH are registered trade marks of
Oxford University Press in the UK and in certain other countries

© Oxford University Press 2010

The moral rights of the author have been asserted

Database right Oxford University Press (maker)

First published 2010

2014 2013 2012 2011 2010

10 9 8 7 6 5 4 3 2 1

ISBN: 978 0 19 482900 7

Printed in China

ACKNOWLEDGEMENTS

The author and publisher would like to thank: Alex Raynham for his contributions
to the Online Workbook.

*The publisher would like to thank the following for permission to reproduce
photographs*: Alamy Images pp.50 (Mt. Cook and Lake Pukaki, New Zealand/
Jon Arnold Images Ltd), 56 (Girl carrying straw/Magdalena Rehova), 72
(Motorway/Ashley Cooper), 73 (Coach/Justin Kase zfourz), 73 (Train station/
PCL), 73 (Ferry/Bill Brooks), 80 (Runner listening to iPod/Harriet Cummings),
100 (pencils/Martin Williams), 103 (Watch/Stephen Mulcahey), 107 (TV
news crew filming/Eddie Gerald); Martin Argles/Guardian News & Media
Ltd 2008 p.6; Axiom Photographic Agency pp.19 (Postcards on stand/Chris
Parker), 67 (Two men wearing hats/J.Sparshatt); Corbis p.8 (Brightly painted
houses/Susan Rosenthal); 9 (Sardinia, Italy/Doug Pearson/JAI), 10 (Robots
sweeping/Volker Moehrke), 43 (Football fans/Colin McPherson), 90 (Dog
sled team/Michael Maslan Historic Photographs); Ellie Farr pp.47 (Beach),
48 (New York); Getty Images pp.12 (Riding bike along wall/Hermann Erber),
16 (Lavender field/Panoramic Images), 20 (Two Yakut girls outdoors/Simon
Roberts), 22 (Killer whales/Chris Cheadle), 23 (Journalist Dan Rather), 27 (Sea
World show/John Warden), 32 (Spectators in floodlight/Ulla Lohmann), 36
(Putting on a ring/Yo), 36 (Photograph of married couple/Riitta Supperi), 38
(Clifton suspension bridge/Panoramic Images), 39 (Holding ice cream cone/
Shannon Fagan), 41 (Woman listening to music/Ryan McVay), 43 (Family
on beach/Roy Mehta), 43 (Crowd of people/John Rowley), 46 (Stingrays/
David Doubilet), 51 (Penguins/Ralph Lee Hopkins), 53 (tiger cubs/Schafer
& Hill/Stone), 53 (airplane/Sami Sarkis/Photographer's Choice), 53 (polar
bear/Sue Flood/The Image Bank), 53 (logging/Keith Douglas/All Canada
Photos), 58 (Sunrise by mountains/monbetsu hokkaido), 62 (Horse riding
on beach at sunset/D H Webster), 68 (View looking up at columns/O. Louis
Mazzatenta), 70 (Huskies pulling sled/Fiona McIntosh), 76 (lechtaler alps/
ingmar wesemann), 82 (*Spiderman* Alain Robert), 91 (Three teenagers lying
in park/James Ross), 92 (Ballet dancer/Yolanda Gonzalez Photography), 96
(Rickshaw/Ed Freeman), 102 (Friends trying on sunglasses/Kathrin Ziegler),
106 (Football commentator/Mike Hewitt); OUP pp.33 (Playing computer
games/Westend61), 33 (Businesswoman/Corbis), 33 (Basketball/Stockbyte),
33 (Group of friends/Pixland), 33 (Beach/Digital Vision), 33 (Expensive car/
Gareth Byrne), 53 (Dead seabirds/Photodisc), 53 (traffic/Digital Vision), 63 (Boy
eating burger/Stockbyte), 83 (Swimmer/Photodisc), 103 (Red car/Corbis), 103
(Mobile phone/Photodisc), 103 (Laptop/David Cook/www.blueshiftstudios.
co.uk), 106 (Weather forecaster/Stockbyte), 107 (Television studio/Corbis);
Photolibrary pp.7 (Female android/Colin Anderson/Blend Images), 18
(Seafood paella/FoodCollection), 23 (Journalist interviewing man/White),
30 (Cellist and violinist/Carlos Davila/White), 33 (Twenty euro notes/Image
Source), 36 (Trophy on grass/Image Source), 36 (Pocket watch/Kim Steele/

White), 43 (Friends having a picnic/White), 57 (Collecting litter on beach/
Cultura), 63 (Woman reading book/Chev Wilkinson/Cultura), 63 (Man alone
in cinema/Image Source), 63 (Woman watching television/Image Source),
63 (Woman with laptop/Image Source), 63 (Woman shopping/Corbis), 73
(Businesswoman boarding plane/Corbis), 83 (Woman eating lettuce/Image
Source), 83 (Mountain biking/Erik Isakson/Tetra Images), 83 (Smoking in
no-smoking area/Radius Images), 83 (Weight training/Stockbroker), 83
(Group doing tai chi/Mike Kemp/Rubberball), 86 (Confused woman/Image
Source), 88 (Girl using laptop/Stockbyte/White), 89 (Teenage girl using laptop/
Ableimages/White), 89 (Friends in tent/Nancy R Cohen/White), 93 (Clubbers
dancing/Amanaimages), 93 (Friends having coffee/Image Source), 93 (Doctor
assisting elderly patient/Corbis), 93 (Grandmother and baby/Rick Gomez/
age fotostock), 103 (Lightbulb/Image Source), 103 (Flat screen television/
Creatas/Comstock); PunchStock pp.53 (landfill/Digital Vision), 87 (Walking on
the beach/Tetra images); Rex Features pp.28 (Johnny Depp in *Public Enemies*/
Universal/Everett), 60 (Flooded town/Sipa Press).

Commissioned illustrations by: Harry Malt pp.26, 52, 95; Patrick Morgan pp.13,
36, 78

Researched illustrations by: Jill Calder pp.14, 35, 61, 87, 101; Harry Malt pp.23,
38, 57, 104, 105; Tim Marrs pp.8, 29, 42, 49, 55, 69, 85, 99; Patrick Morgan
pp.13, 24, 45, 65, 75

*The author and publisher are grateful to those who have given permission to reproduce
the following extracts of copyright material*: p.6 From '250 Huns? No Problem!' by
Will Hodgkinson, 13 February 2008, *The Guardian*. Copyright Guardian News
& Media Ltd, 2008. Reproduced by permission; p.10 From 'How toddlers can
help us to build more human robots' by Laura Parker, 14 February 2008,
Technology Guardian Inside IT. Copyright Guardian News & Media Ltd, 2008.
Reproduced by permission; p.20 From 'Language cull could leave people
speechless' by David Ward, 25 May 2002, *The Guardian*. Copyright Guardian
News & Media Ltd, 2002; p.30 From 'And the band played badly' by Alexander
McCall Smith, 12 March 2008, *International Herald Tribune* © 2009 The New
York Times (Distributed by The New York Times Syndicate). Reproduced
by permission; p.36-37 From *The Means of Escape* by Penelope Fitzgerald.
Reprinted by permission of HarperCollins Publishers Ltd. © Penelope
Fitzgerald, 2000; p.46 From 'One hell of a paradise' by Philip Moore, April
2002, British Airways *High Life Magazine*. Reproduced by kind permission
of the author; p.67 From 'Going local' by Vicky Baker, 15 March 2008, *The
Guardian Travel*. Copyright Guardian News & Media Ltd, 2008. Reproduced
by permission; p.70 From 'Going to the dogs' by Jon Ronson, 1 March
2008, *The Guardian Weekend*. Copyright Guardian News & Media Ltd, 2008.
Reproduced by permission; p.76 From *Rambling on the road to Rome* by Peter
Francis Browne. Reproduced by permission of Peter Francis Browne; p.86
From 'Private lives: Our flatmate won't do his washing-up' by Linda Blair, 28
February 2008, *The Guardian*. Copyright Guardian News & Media Ltd, 2008.
Reproduced by permission; p.90 From 'How teamwork saved Alaska' from
winter/spring edition of *CNN Traveller Magazine*. Reproduced by permission;
p.96 From 'China's young artists well schooled in market savvy' by David
Barboza, 2 April 2008, *International Herald Tribune* © 2009 The New York Times
(Distributed by The New York Times Syndicate). Reproduced by permission;
p.100 From 'Ask Leo – Your ethical dilemmas sorted' by Leo Hickman, 13
March 2008, *The Guardian*. Copyright Guardian News & Media Ltd, 2008.
Reproduced by permission

*Although every effort has been made to trace and contact copyright holders before
publication, this has not been possible in some cases. We apologize for any apparent
infringement of copyright and if notified, the publisher will be pleased to rectify any
errors or omissions at the earliest opportunity.*